Praise for *bulletproof*

'Yes yes yes! Finally, a book that doesn't say resilience is about having a positive mindset. Instead, it explains the role our mind plays in how we approach life. Simple, myth busting and life changing. An all round brilliant book!'

Victoria Humphries, polar adventurer; 3x Guinness world record holder; resilience specialist and inspirational speaker

'What Chantal Burns shares in this book is genuinely life changing. If you want to navigate life with more ease and less mental noise, read this book and it will show you how.'

Julie Lavington, Founder and CEO, Sosandar

'This is the book I wish I'd had when I was young and full of fear . . . continuously wounded by the bullets of my thinking. This book is as useful and practical as a "spiritual" book can get!'

Steve Chandler, author of *Time Warrior*

'With her characteristic humour and insight, and her ability to draw from all fields, Chantal Burns has written the book we all need now, from global and corporate leaders to grassroots activists and everyone in between. We can each contribute to positive change on Earth, but we must understand how positive and sustainable change happens in each one of us first.'

Ami Chen Mills, author of *The Spark Inside* and *State of Mind in the* Classroom; host of the *Moment of Truth with Ami Chen Mills* radio show and podcast

'I have shared Chantal Burns' first book, *Instant Motivation*, with all the leaders I coach. When people understand the logic of how their minds work, they are free from limiting thoughts and open to insight that gives rise to deep and lasting change. Now in her excellent new book, Chantal challenges many of the myths that stop us from connecting with our most creative and transformative asset – innate resilience. If you're a coach, counsellor, psychologist or just someone who wants to help yourself and others to live and lead well, this book is essential. Read it and then give a copy to your clients.'

Dr Cheryl Bond, Senior Faculty, Conscious Leadership School

'In a world where words like resilience, mindfulness, and well-being are often overused and misunderstood, Chantal Burns sets the record straight. With simplicity and clarity, she brings us back to the true essence of resilience. Enriched with amusing and helpful images and quotations, *bulletproof* manages to redefine well-worn concepts in an innovative and soul-stirring manner. Even if you are somewhat familiar with this subject, you will find an enlightening perspective within these pages.'

Nick Hammond, Charity Chair of Trustees; mindfulness teacher and TED speaker

'*bulletproof* doesn't ask you to reject patterns of thought or adopt an artificial new construct for life. Instead it has that very rare ability to assist you in reframing and re-evaluating existing thought and emotion in wholly unexpected and positive ways. We are resilient, but it takes a powerful tome such as this to enable you to embrace this deeper truth. Everyone should read this book.'

Jezz Vernon, film producer; Senior Lecturer at University of Exeter

'If you think you know how reality works, think again. *bulletproof* is an excellent book that will surprise you and may well challenge everything you thought you knew about resilience. And the ultimate prize? Realising that we already have the essential qualities we need if we want to live well, be brave and create a beautiful life.'

Chris Ingham, Director of Business Excellence; Conscious Leadership School Graduate

'Do you assume that time itself heals all wounds? Do you always give a thumbs-up to positive thinking? Do you take getting upset at the state of the world to mean that there is something wrong with you or your feelings? If you have answered "yes" to any of these questions, then you need to read this! Because Burns' *bulletproof* expertly and practically challenges such assumptions as these and more. The result? Turn toxic positivity into radical resilience for a better future.'

Dr. Rupert Read, author of *Parents For A Future: How Loving Our Children Can Prevent Climate Collapse*

'Reading this book feels like having a conversation with a friend, and then BOOM, you hear something that hits you between the eyes. *bulletproof* manages to strike that rare balance between being light and deep, and ordinary and profound. Unlike most books on this subject, you won't find a long list of strategies to fix yourself. Turns out you don't need fixing. And you don't need to think or feel a certain way to be resilient. The book's core message is that we come into the world with an unbreakable spirit of resilience. So you can breathe a sigh of relief and live your life of ups and downs with compassion and grace.'

Sandra Krot, Human Dimension Consultant; co-author of *Invisible Power: Insight Principles at Work*

'This is an unusual take on resilience. In *bulletproof*, Chantal busts some harmful myths and illuminates the ill effects of cultural conditioning when responding to life challenges. In essence, it is a manual for how to explore the depths of your soul without getting lost. It's a fantastic and brave book that invites new insights that enable you to use your mind more wisely. After all, that's what resilience is really about.'

Villö Lelkes, Head of Water Emergencies, Water Security and Resilience, DEFRA

'Chantal's book is a brilliant and practical guide to what it truly means to be emotionally resilient. But it's also about hope, inspiration and redefining our ideas about who we are and what we can accomplish. To realise that we have it within ourselves to change, without being limited by our ideas, beliefs and past experiences, is empowering. And it removes our excuses!'

Russell Brown, Chief Financial Officer, SoPost

'No matter how messy life gets, *bulletproof* shows you how to keep calm, carry on, get sh*t done and feel great doing it! To know that whatever comes our way, we already have everything we need is a game changer and that's what this book will give you.'

Hannah Carter, CEO and Founder, OGGS

'Wonderful insight into the inside-out principle behind life. Chantal weaves personal stories with practical exercises and wide reference sources to make this book an absolute gem! Read it and see for yourself!'

Bridget Marrison, Head of Communications, Spadework; Yoga teacher

'Chantal's book masterfully helps reveal your inner wisdom, offering insightful and practical guidance. A true companion, *bulletproof* is an invaluable addition to your side table, always ready to shift your perspective whenever you need it.'

Marcela Tarazona, PhD, Head of Climate and Economics,
Genesis Analytics

'If you're looking for a fresh approach to resilience and mental wellbeing this book delivers it. Chantal Burns unravels common misconceptions of what resilience is (and isn't) and offers a life-changing guide to inner security and empowerment. Through her simple, accessible and passionate distillation of some pretty big psychological theories, she opens up a clear route for the reader to rediscover their innate strengths and wisdom. I've read it twice and I know I'll keep going back to it.

If you think your mental health is being challenged, or you've been feeling up against it, whether in your personal or professional life, this is the book for you. I wish it had been written 20 years ago!'

Justine Southall, advisor and former MD of
***Marie Claire* magazine**

'Just WOW! I read *bulletproof* in one sitting - couldn't put it down. There is wisdom dripping off every page. I found insights relevant to my today, my yesterday, and my tomorrow. I could hear my own voice reverberating in the stories. It's given me so much clarity. I'm going in for a second read and I will be recommending this book to everyone I know.'

Sarah Messer, Managing Director, Nielsen Research

'In *bulletproof* Chantal Burns shares a simple but powerful truth. With great simplicity, she shines a light on the wisdom and qualities we already hold within. Expertly blending stories with practical exploration, unhelpful beliefs are released, allowing you to re-focus your mental energy, and be guided to clarity of perspective, action and ultimately a more fulfilling life.'

Tom Probert, Head of Marketing, Meridian Energy Ltd

'*bulletproof* is an essential guide to living a courageous and compassionate life. Chantal Burns brings a wealth of wisdom and insight as she dismantles old ideas about thought and reality. With lots of great examples, she shows us why the qualities of resilience aren't something that we have to build or practice, because they're already inside. We just need to learn what gets in the way. A brilliant book that you can revisit whenever you need a reset.'

**Josh Krichefski, CEO GroupM EMEA and UK;
mental health advocate**

'My hat goes off to Chantal Burns. *bulletproof* not only demythologises the subject of resilience but, if you look carefully, she demonstrates a deeper logic that can be applied to all aspects of life. This book does not add further layers of confusion to our understanding of mental life. To the contrary, she strips it away, and reveals resilience to be the truth of our nature and our saving grace.'

Dr Keith Blevens, Clinical Psychologist and educator

'*bulletproof* expertly reveals the unexpected source of resilience each person carries within them. As we face a humanitarian crisis in mental health, this clear, accessible book carries fresh hope for readers in every walk of life, regardless of what you've been through and what you're up against. Chantal Burns' excellent book uncovers the wisdom and wellbeing we all need to thrive in the volatile and complex times we're living through. Highly recommended.'

**Jamie Smart, *Sunday Times* bestselling author,
speaker and coach**

'*bulletproof* is an exceptional exploration into the true source of resilience. Every page has a new insight that will change lives if we embrace the deeper logic being shared. Chantal Burns brings empathy, humour, and profound wisdom, creating a wonderful blend of personal anecdotes, practical guidance, and illuminating research. She challenges you to rethink your perceptions in a way that feels personal, as if she is speaking with you, but is universally relevant.

This book will help people to break free from unhelpful patterns and limitations. It is literally like having the scales lifted from your eyes when you fully grasp the grounding principle of *bulletproof*. It should be required reading for everyone who wants to free their mind and help others do the same.'

**Dawn Hewitt, CEO- CHUMS Child Bereavement, Trauma and
Emotional Wellbeing Service**

bulletproof

Pearson

At Pearson, we have a simple mission: to help people make more of their lives through learning.

We combine innovative learning technology with trusted content and educational expertise to provide engaging and effective learning experiences that serve people wherever and whenever they are learning.

From classroom to boardroom, our curriculum materials, digital learning tools and testing programmes help to educate millions of people worldwide – more than any other private enterprise.

Every day our work helps learning flourish, and wherever learning flourishes, so do people.

To learn more, please visit us at **www.pearson.com**

bulletproof

Be fearless and resilient – no matter what

Chantal Burns

Pearson

Harlow, England • London • New York • Boston • San Francisco • Toronto • Sydney
Dubai • Singapore • Hong Kong • Tokyo • Seoul • Taipei • New Delhi
Cape Town • São Paulo • Mexico City • Madrid • Amsterdam • Munich • Paris • Milan

PEARSON EDUCATION LIMITED

KAO Two
KAO Park
Harlow CM17 9NA
United Kingdom
Tel: +44 (0)1279 623623
Web: www.pearson.com

First edition published 2024 (print and electronic)

ISBN: 978-1-292-33002-0 (print)
          978-1-292-33004-4 (ePub)

British Library Cataloguing-in-Publication Data
A catalogue record for the print edition is available from the British Library

Library of Congress Cataloging-in-Publication Data
Names: Burns, Chantal, author.
Title: Bulletproof : be fearless and resilient, no matter what / Chantal
    Burns.
Description: First edition. | Harlow, England ; New York : Pearson, 2024. |
    Includes bibliographical references and index.
Identifiers: LCCN 2023051110 | ISBN 9781292330020 (paperback) | ISBN
    9781292330044 (epub)
Subjects: LCSH: Resilience (Personality trait) | Courage.
Classification: LCC BF698.35.R47 B87 2024 | DDC 155.2/4--dc23/eng/20231116
LC record available at https://lccn.loc.gov/2023051110

10 9 8 7 6 5 4 3 2 1
28 27 26 25 24

Cover design by Kelly Miller
Cover image: StarLineArts/iStock/Getty

Print edition typeset in 10/14 Charter ITC Pro by Straive

NOTE THAT ANY PAGE CROSS REFERENCES REFER TO THE PRINT EDITION

For my beautiful Mum
who showed me
love and courage every day

Contents

Contents

Pearson's Commitment to Diversity, Equity and Inclusion

Pearson is dedicated to creating bias-free content that reflects the diversity, depth and breadth of all learners' lived experiences. We embrace the many dimensions of diversity including, but not limited to, race, ethnicity, gender, sex, sexual orientation, socioeconomic status, ability, age and religious or political beliefs.

Education is a powerful force for equity and change in our world. It has the potential to deliver opportunities that improve lives and enable economic mobility. As we work with authors to create content for every product and service, we acknowledge our responsibility to demonstrate inclusivity and incorporate diverse scholarship so that everyone can achieve their potential through learning. As the world's leading learning company, we have a duty to help drive change and live up to our purpose to help more people create a better life for themselves and to create a better world.

Our ambition is to purposefully contribute to a world where:

- Everyone has an equitable and lifelong opportunity to succeed through learning.
- Our educational products and services are inclusive and represent the rich diversity of learners.
- Our educational content accurately reflects the histories and lived experiences of the learners we serve.
- Our educational content prompts deeper discussions with students and motivates them to expand their own learning and worldview.

We are also committed to providing products that are fully accessible to all learners. As per Pearson's guidelines for accessible educational Web media, we test and retest the capabilities of our products against the highest standards for every release, following the WCAG guidelines in developing new products for copyright year 2022 and beyond. You can learn more about Pearson's commitment to accessibility at:

https://www.pearson.com/us/accessibility.html

What this book
is not about

Just a mention of the word resilience and eyes often roll. Many of us feel like we're already at capacity, just about holding it together. And along comes another book telling you to be resilient. But I promise this is different.

Despite what we get told, true resilience isn't about putting on a brave face or toughing it out. It's about acknowledging reality without suppressing your feelings or pretending 'everything's fine'. It's not about constantly pushing yourself to be more or striving for impossible perfection. It's about being yourself and knowing when to rest or when to quit.

This book aims to shatter every major myth and misunderstanding about resilience. Because it's these compelling illusions that cloud your clarity, stop you speaking up, steal your joy and fuel insecurity and chronic stress.

Imagine if you could think clearly, face reality without denial, speak your truth and be compassionate with yourself and others, *no matter what.* In other words, what if you are bulletproof in all the ways that matter most?

And we need this because, let's be honest, there's a lot going on. It's easy to feel mentally hijacked by day-to-day stuff, let alone the bigger issues beyond our front door. From political and economic turbulence, an environmental crisis through to social injustice and war, the world seems increasingly unstable. As a friend poetically described, 'it's a bit of a shit-show'.

Where there are humans, there is insecurity, fear and oppression. But there's also an abundance of courage, clarity, lightness and love. So, how do we get more of that?

'The crisis is not out there in the world; it is within our own consciousness.'

Krishnamurti, spiritual teacher and author

The more we understand our inner world, the more we can break free from deceptive thought traps, clear the clutter and function freely, without fear in the driving seat. And this automatically changes how we relate and respond to people, systems, communities and the natural world that we are inseparable from.

With a free mind, we can face our fears, make difficult decisions, have honest conversations, and live well together, without unnecessary suffering.

> ## Useful distinction:
> ### what to *think* versus how *Thought* works
>
> There are thousands of products about dieting but, despite all the great advice and strategies, in many parts of the world, we have an obesity epidemic. There are also thousands of self-help books, podcasts, videos or apps and over 500 different psychological therapies and, yet, we still have a mental health crisis in many societies. So, instead of giving you more advice and telling you what to think or feel, we're going behind the scenes to explore how the mind works and why having this awareness and insight holds the key to your emotional resilience and mental well-being.

The power of realisation

Information without realisation is like eating without digesting. Anyone can share a fact with you, but it's only when we grasp its deeper meaning or feel touched by its gravity, that a fact transforms into embodied understanding. And that's when real change happens.

And the best part is that we're born with the power to realise, think again and change our minds. When you think about it, everything you've learned and will learn is the result of countless insights or realisations, big and small. It's when confusion becomes clarity or solutions suddenly appear out of nowhere. It's when you go from feeling lost to feeling at home in yourself. It's those moments when your heart and mind shift so fundamentally, that you are forever changed.

> **'There is only one real knowledge; that which helps us to be free. Every other type of knowledge is just mere amusement.'**
>
> **Vishnu Purana, Indian wisdom[1]**

The only barrier to mental freedom is how we innocently get in our own way. For example, I always thought I was open minded and willing to have my thinking challenged. It turns out I was more interested in being right or proving myself than I was in hearing something new.

It can feel scary to let go of longstanding ideas and beliefs, especially if they're tied to your sense of identity or if that way of thinking has helped you in the past. But when you get curious about what you don't yet know, it opens the door to new possibilities and new realities. After all, can you ever say that you've had every new thought there is to think? ☺

Being *bulletproof* is not just a motivational bumper sticker

Your soul or spirit . . . the very essence of who you are *is* unbreakable. That's why you can get back up after being knocked down. It's why you can face fear without being defeated by it. It's why you are still here, right now . . . despite break ups, breakdowns, epic fails, loss, heartache, or any other challenges that you've faced in your life.

So, if you want to live fearlessly, with more joy, compassion, courage and clarity, and help others do the same, this book has been written for you.

Before you dive into Chapter 1, check out your free online gift below to get some useful insight as you journey through this book.

Get your online State of Mind Index (SOMi): This is free and easy to complete. Just scan this QR code or use the link below.

http://www.chantalburns.com/bulletproof-somi-stateofmindindex/

One more thing! If you love listening to music when you're reading, here's what I played while writing.

www.okiemofficial.com
Xiro and The Golden Circle by Okiem.

Plus The Tape by Martha Tilston, Our Generation by Tokio Myers, Vangelis, Art of Noise, Groove Armada, Air, Daft Punk and Moby.

part 1

What resilience is and how it really works

chapter 1

The resilience myth

'It ain't what you don't know that gets you into trouble.
It's what you know for sure that just ain't so.'

Mark Twain

It was June 2011, just three months after the huge earthquake and tsunami in Japan that killed nearly twenty thousand people, devastating many communities. The full magnitude of loss was immeasurable.

I was due to teach in Tokyo, but frequent aftershocks meant my seminars were moved to Osaka to reduce risk of disruption. I met people and listened to their stories, struck by the range of reactions to what had happened. Some were in shock, feeling hopeless and depressed, unable to engage in anything. Many were mobilising communities, and finding deeper levels of connection, meaning and purpose.

Have you ever wondered how some people keep going when times are tough, while others seem more easily defeated, or how you can stay calm in a crisis but have a total meltdown over something trivial? What makes us cling to the comfort of familiarity when, at other times, we take risks or embrace the unknown? And what part does personality, environment and upbringing play in our resilience?

These are some of the questions I want to shed light on.

I'm sure, like me, you have moments when you feel invincible and ready to take on the world and other times, when tying your shoelaces feels like an Olympic sport.

Life is full of twists and turns. It's messy and unpredictable. We're going to face all kinds of situations, big and small, that require courage, clarity, creativity and compassion. I don't know about you, but sometimes it feels like all four have left the building.

In an article by Ann Masten,[1] a developmental psychologist and researcher, she says:

'Resilience does not come from rare and special qualities, but from the everyday magic of ordinary, normative human resources in the minds, brains and bodies of children.'[2]

It's this ordinary magic that helps you move mountains and keep going even when it feels like all the odds are stacked against you or there's nothing left in the tank.

The mind is a formidable force. It opens the door to new possibilities but closes it just as quickly. Even when long-held beliefs are proven untrue, we have a knack of convincing ourselves otherwise. And, with the rise of fake news, AI and self-appointed experts, it's crucial to question what you hear and listen to your own wisdom.

In this book, I'll debunk the major myths about resilience that can leave you feeling stuck or powerless. When false ideas fall away, it frees you up. And what we most need is a free mind, so here's an overview of these myths to set the scene.

Myth 1: We need to build emotional resilience

As a species, we've evolved over millions of years, and we keep showing how adaptable we are. Every day, people solve what seem like insurmountable problems. I've no doubt that when faced with hardship, you've been able to find inner strength and creativity, even if it's taken you by surprise.

So instead of thinking about resilience as something we should build, develop or practise, what if we just need to uncover it? What if resilience is the *nature* of nature . . . the nature of *you*?

This brings us to the next one . . .

Myth 2: Some people are more resilient than others

On a BBC news programme during the Covid pandemic, a well-known comedian and mental health advocate said 'some people are born resilient, it's in the genes'. This implies that not everyone has this resource within, which isn't true but it's a common misconception.

Courage isn't genetic and there are no pre-determined levels of spiritual and psychological wellness. Along with your own examples, there's evidence all around us that resilience is always available, regardless of genes, personality or any other factor. But like the sun on a cloudy day, sometimes our resilience gets hidden, which is why it's helpful to learn what gets in the way and how to uncover it. More about this later.

Myth 3: Resilience only shows itself in times of trauma

Life dishes up daily challenges, changes, decisions or setbacks, whether it's finding a job, training for a marathon, being a parent, dealing with loss, getting over break-ups, managing finances or handling health issues.

I've had to face my fears or dig deep to find that extra dose of determination. No doubt, you've got your own examples too. When you think about it, any change or situation that disrupts the norm, breaks new ground or requires new skills, inevitably needs strength of spirit. And that's not something that only shows up in specific moments. Like the sun, resilience is a constant that you can always rely on, even when you can't see or feel it.

Myth 4: Resilience means being tough

Being unwaveringly strong and not showing vulnerability is linked to old gender norms and patriarchal structures throughout history. These old ideas tend to stigmatise emotional expression, framing it as 'weak'. This leads to pretending, denying and detaching as a way to cope. And this fosters more suffering, not less. But when we embrace the fullness of the human experience, including moments of struggle, we find our freedom.

Linked to this . . .

Myth 5: Resilience comes from controlling your emotions

One of the most damaging misconceptions is that being resilient means managing your mental state. This myth is founded on two false ideas; the first, that we can control what we feel and, the second, that feelings are a problem to be fixed.

We're encouraged to 'think positive' and avoid negative feelings, which only creates more mental noise. Today's Western societies tend to pathologise and medicate natural emotions, evidenced by the surge in prescribed antidepressants and anxiety drugs.

> **'To demedicalise distress is not to delegitimise distress. One can honor, respect and care for profound suffering without labelling it as illness, pathology or disorder.'**
>
> **James Davies, PhD[3]**

When we misdiagnose the source and nature of feelings, we end up looking in the wrong place, trying to control or fix something in ourselves or others that cannot be controlled and cannot be broken.

What if you didn't have to change or escape uncomfortable feelings? What if thriving didn't depend on being in a 'better' state of mind?

Whatever your current emotional state, psychological health always exists. More about this in future chapters.

Myth 6: Adversity = Distress

It's commonly assumed that hardship or toxic events will inevitably cause suffering or distress. In her landmark book,[4] Dr Marilyn Bowman says, "The prevailing model used by clinical psychologists, psychiatrists, and other MH professionals predicts that toxic events will normally trigger clinically significant distress symptoms." Yet, hundreds of studies on people's response to extreme adversity shows that events in and of themselves have no automatic or predetermined impact.

One example is a study that tracked 775 soldiers returning home after the Persian Gulf war, where 13% were diagnosed with PTSD (post-traumatic stress disorder) while the majority (62%), had no sign of psychological distress. If not for upbringing, genetics or environment, what accounts for these differences?

Researchers have identified that 'innate qualities' are the key to how we respond to situations including exposure to war.[5] We'll explore these qualities and what gets in the way of them in future chapters.

Myth 7: Life is happening *to* you

Linked to the previous myth is the major misconception that the past or future can dictate how we feel, respond and act in the present.

If this were true, a person who loses a child would be forever trapped in sorrow but many families are able to rediscover joy, despite profound loss. And, if the dark shadow of a traumatic past could determine someone's future, they would never find the light again, yet countless survivors of abuse are able to heal and find peace.

It's true that we can feel like we've lost our way. At times, we might feel broken or believe we can't handle what we're facing. I've had my share of those moments. But how you think or feel in any moment does not make you any less resilient at your core.

These myths that have troubled humanity by keeping us stuck in false beliefs and insecurity, stem from a compelling illusion that sits at the heart of this book:

The mother of all myths: We live in two worlds

Ever feel like you're living in two different worlds at the same time? There's an inner world of thoughts, feelings and sensations, and there's an outer world of situations, people, nature, objects. It's easy to think that these two worlds are separate when, in reality, the outside world cannot exist without an inner world that creates and perceives it. It's one world, one life. And, when we get a sense of this, it changes everything. You begin to understand and relate to yourself, other people and everything around you in a totally different way.

And the best part is how it frees you from fear and insecurity that comes from feeling controlled by an external world. It's like discovering a superpower that's been inside all along.

To sum up this first chapter, here's what resilience means in the context of our time together.

Resilience *is not:*

- stiff upper lip
- forced optimism, wishful thinking or putting a positive spin on things
- something you have to practise or build
- mental toughness
- control
- avoiding, denying or fixing your feelings
- a personal accomplishment
- physical

Resilience *is:*

- ♥ pre-existing
- ♥ spiritual energy
- ♥ unconditional
- ♥ mental freedom
- ♥ unbreakable
- ♥ wholeness
- ♥ love
- ♥ your true nature.

Over the course of your life, resilience has shown itself in countless ways. Whether it's getting through hardship, finding answers, healing from heart break, speaking out, making changes, helping others, or setting clear boundaries. It's when find yourself in fierce waters, feeling out of your depth but knowing you can stay afloat and find your way home.

In essence, *you are bulletproof.*

chapter 2

It's an inside>out world

'Reality is that which when you stop believing in it, doesn't go away.'

Philip K. Dick

If you knew without doubt that emotional security and a free mind was always available and could never be taken from you, what would this mean for how you live your life?

'I would take more risks . . . I would be more compassionate . . . I would feel free to say what I think . . . I wouldn't worry so much . . . ' were some of the answers when I posed this question at a conference.

And when I asked the management team of a mental health charity the same question, one of their trauma specialists said, 'This *is* resilience . . . if you know this, you can feel psychologically secure, no matter what.'

This gets to the heart of the book. No matter what has happened, is happening, or might happen in the future, your spirit, the essence of 'you', is unbreakable by its very nature.

Professor of clinical psychology, George A. Bonanno[1] has spent over 25 years researching resilience with a focus on trauma and loss. One study looked at rates of depression among people hospitalised with spinal cord injuries. They found that 'the majority showed almost no depression' and were 'not any more depressed than the average person'.

Does this seem surprising? It's generally assumed that people who live through this kind of experience are more likely to struggle with their mental health. There's plenty of evidence to back up this assumption but, crucially, you can also find evidence that disproves it.

In another study, children living under wartime conditions of constant shelling and bombardment near the Jordan border were compared to children living in an area without these conditions. The researchers expected to see a significant difference in anxiety and other symptoms but didn't find any. Similarly, children brought up in difficult or dangerous circumstances, including abuse or alcoholism, are often shown to have as much hardiness and adaptability as children with no significant adversity.[2]

This isn't to say that children don't experience anxiety, distress or other psychological symptoms, or that these feelings and responses aren't warranted or valid. But it does mean that it's not predetermined or inevitable.

In addition to their own studies including the 9/11 terrorist attack and the SARS epidemic, Bonnano and his team reviewed research on how people respond to abuse, bereavement, injury, loss, chronic pain, divorce, cancer and combat exposure. The most common response is resilience, meaning that, despite exposure to difficult or life-threatening events, people can regain or maintain healthy psychological and physical functioning.

History is littered with powerful examples of how we rise up, overcome and use our collective wisdom and compassion to make things right. And every day, in our own communities, we find examples of how the most common response to difficulty is not defeat but strength of spirit.

Dr Marilyn Bowman is no stranger to adversity. She survived two collapsed lungs at 17, tuberculosis at 23 and regular attacks of relapsing-remitting MS from the age of 37. After she retired, she was diagnosed with breast cancer. Despite the many serious threats to her health, she talks about life as a series of adventures and lives in gratitude.

Throughout her career as a clinical psychologist and researcher, she observed a huge variety of responses to hardship. She was curious about what accounts for these differences, so she began to investigate the commonly held assumption that life events automatically lead to psychological distress.

When I came across her work, I was intrigued by her avoidance of the term 'traumatic event', instead using the word 'toxic'.[3] When

I asked her about this, she said, 'I really want to avoid describing events as traumatic because trauma is what the person decides they are experiencing. It doesn't describe the event itself.'

I needed to reflect on this. My friend is a trauma specialist. She works with people who have been abused or tortured. Could this really apply to them?

After a rigorous review of over 500 studies, Dr Bowman's significant finding was that adversity *does not* equal distress.[4] For example, there are people who report no major hardship in their lives, yet they suffer with crippling anxiety. And there are people who have been through life-threatening situations and report no symptoms of PTSD or long-term pathology.

Another striking example is 'second-hand' trauma, where someone *hears* about an event without having any direct exposure to it and then develops symptoms of PTSD themselves.[5]

How do we account for these experiences? What's really going on?

It's evident that how we interpret and respond to hardship plays a central role in our emotional well-being and resilience, so let's dig a little deeper on this.

The power in perceiving

Right now, what can you see?
Tune into any sounds. What can you hear?
Notice any sensations. What can you feel?

You might think that you're observing an objective reality that exists 'out there', independent from and separate to you . . . as if your mind is simply a camera recording what it's witnessing and sensing. But, as I shared in my first book[6] . . .

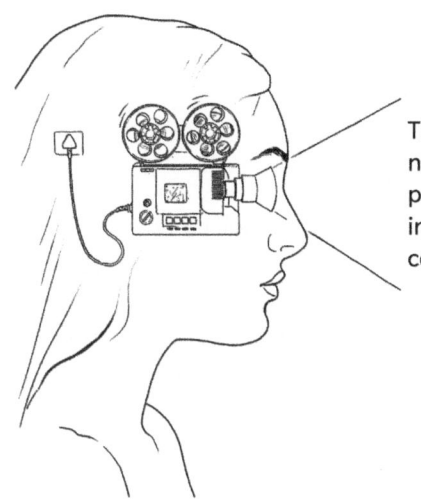

The mind is like a projector, not a camera, and what you are perceiving and experiencing in each moment, is your own consciousness projected outwards.

I love walking in the countryside. I'm always struck by the vibrant colours, the scents of summer or that satisfying crunch of leaves under your feet. It's easy to take this all for granted but, without the creative power of your mind, you wouldn't be able to experience these sights, sounds, smells and feels.

For example, colour doesn't exist as a separate entity out there. Instead, your eyes are detecting a dance of light waves, as your mind turns them into the colours you see.

And right now, your ears are detecting vibrations in the air, while your mind interprets them as sound. How wild is that!

In his widely watched Ted Talk, neuroscientist Anil Seth said: *'We don't just passively perceive the world, we actively create it.'*[7]

In other words, life is an inside>out experience.

Thought experiments

Hermann grid illusion

You can create this yourself by drawing a grid of black squares on a white background, similar to a chess board. Keep a consistent amount of space between them. And then look at the grid and notice if you see anything else appearing.

If you see grey spots, are they really there or is your mind creating them?

Checker shadow illusion

Look at this image below and compare the squares marked A and B. Are they the same shade or not?

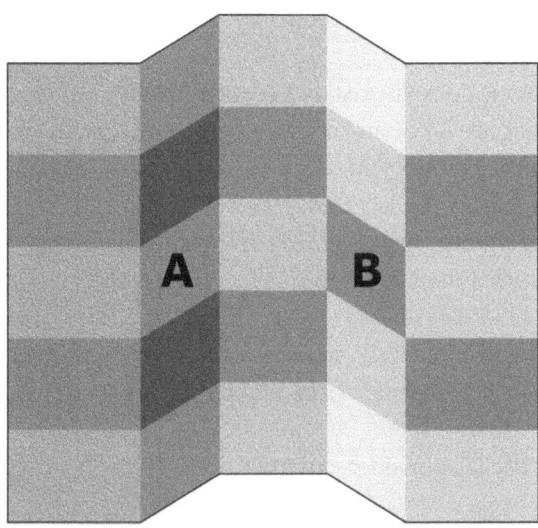

They are in fact exactly the same shade but your mind perceives them as different.

Here's how it looks when you take away all the surrounding elements, except those two boxes.

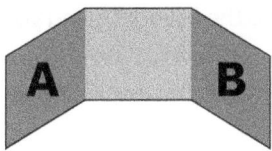

Now take a look at the central three columns numbered 1, 2 and 3. Are they protruding towards you or away from you?

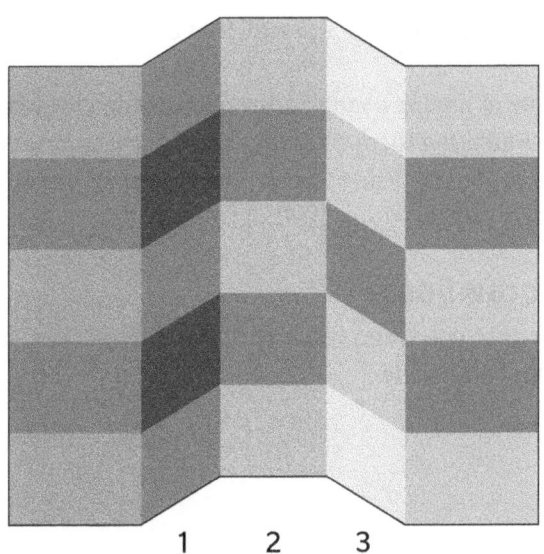

In reality, the columns are neither protruding nor receding. They're not doing anything. They only exist because your mind is creating and perceiving them in a particular way.

Take a bite

Imagine your favourite food in vivid detail – see the colours, feel the texture, remember the smell. And now imagine taking a bite . . . savouring the taste as you notice the flavours filling your mouth.

What physical sensations are you aware of?

As soon as I imagine my favourite meal, my mouth immediately starts to water.

On the other hand, the slightest thought of rice pudding used to make me gag, thanks to (memories of) being forced to eat it at school. A few years ago, as an experiment I decided to live life on the edge and give it another go. Holding my nose, I took a tiny mouthful and was shocked to discover it wasn't that bad.

It reminds me of having a major crush on someone for years, only to realise, after meeting them, that they were nothing like the person I had cooked up in my head ☺ Such is the power of imagination and conditioning.

Creepy crawlies

What happens to you when you look at this image? Or if I ask you to imagine a big hairy spider?

When we show similar images to groups during our programmes, we get a range of reactions. Some people's fear response is so intense they refuse to look. Some leave the room and will only return when the image has been removed. The interesting thing is that most of these people haven't had any kind of 'bad spider experience' to report. They can't explain their reaction apart from saying things like, 'Just looking at one makes me feel scared.'

Mention the word *banana* within earshot of my friend Debi and she goes bananas. And it's not because she's allergic to them. It's just that, in her mind, this humble fruit is the work of the devil.

Placebo is another example of the mind's power. In a study, elite cyclists took cornflower capsules believing it was a new performance-enhancing supplement. Despite being fatigued from their time trials earlier that day, they raced again and set a new personal best, exceeding their own expectations.

What's so interesting with placebo is that, even when people are told they are taking a sugar pill instead of active medication, studies show that many of these patients still report improvements. How come?

Research into the effectiveness of anti-depressants using placebo has shown that a person's expectations are often the active ingredient in improving their mental health.[8] Another fascinating example is with people who have Parkinson's disease. Brain scans of those who received placebo 'treatment' shows brain activity that mirrors those receiving the active medication designed to alleviate symptoms.

So, this is fascinating stuff but how does it relate to emotional/ psychological resilience?

The cause–effect confusion

Most of us know that our mind plays a major role in our experience of life. For example, 81% of respondents to our study said their state of mind was crucial for doing well at work.[9] But have you ever wondered how your mood can so easily fluctuate from moment to moment or day to day? For example, one moment you're feeling completely at ease then, a few minutes later, you're consumed by a wave of anxiety. There's no obvious trigger, just a noticeable shift in your emotional or physical state.

When we ask people, 'What do you think most influences your state of mind?', reasons include upbringing, past situations, weather, the future, workload, social media, genes, how people treat me, whether things go to plan . . .

We think someone's words or deeds can destroy our confidence, that sunny weather can magically change our mood or that a crap journey to work can ruin our day. It can seem like there's an endless list of things that can build us up or tear us down. And that means there's a lot to think about or deal with. It's no wonder we get so mentally overwhelmed.

But what if there's a simpler explanation that we're overlooking? What if we are assigning power to things that cannot be the cause of our psychological experience? And, if that's true, imagine the time and energy you'll get back ☺

For over 25 years, I've helped thousands of people think differently and improve their lives. But I noticed a pattern. As one issue got resolved, they would return with another one to fix. On paper, it might seem like a great business model – you never run out of work – but I couldn't shake the feeling that we were missing something.

When there's an endless list of possible causes for our ever-changing feelings, the search never stops and neither do people's unresolved issues, including my own.

I kept searching and studying, accumulating more and more techniques and strategies. My toolkit was bursting at the seams. I could barely keep track of it all. And still I didn't feel like we were getting to the heart of the issues. Then, in 2009, I was introduced to a new understanding of the mind that made sense of everything.

I realised we were putting buckets under leaky pipes instead of repairing the plumbing. In other words, we were alleviating psychological symptoms without getting to the root cause.

Imagine if every emotion, sensation, perception and behaviour can be traced back to three fundamental forces of nature . . . forces that represent the underlying mechanisms governing your entire mental life.

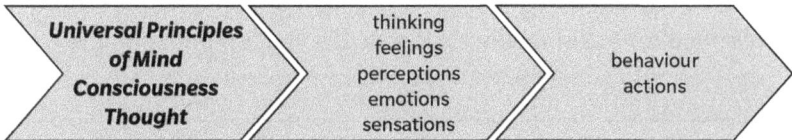

Before philosopher Sydney Banks uncovered these principles in the 1970s, the idea of life being an inside>out reality had been explored in many forms for millennia, through science, fiction, philosophy, poetry, art and religion.

For example, the Buddhist concept of 'Maya' likens the mind to a master illusionist, shaping your personal reality using thought and consciousness. And ancient Greek philosophers taught us that emotions arise from our judgements or desires and not from events themselves. It was said that by understanding the natural order of things, you can find a state of unconditional inner peace.

To read more about Sydney Banks' inspirational story with first-hand accounts from practitioners who studied with him, plus other useful materials, see 'The journey continues' later in the book.

Useful distinction:
first principles vs personal principles

Personal principles (beliefs, ethics, values etc.) are like clothes – you can ditch or update them any time. But a first principle is an unchanging, universal fact of nature. Think gravity. You can deny its existence, but if you drop a glass, it will nosedive every time because it's a scientific principle.

In the same way, *Mind*, *Thought* and *Consciousness* are constant forces shaping our reality. They're like the backstage crew in a theatre. You might not see them but they're always running the show.

We can debate the principles of *Thought* or *Consciousness*, but we would be using them to do that. It's like fish debating the existence of water while they're swimming in it.

'Mental functioning cannot possibly exist without these three psychological elements. They are the building blocks of all mental behaviour. They create all human experience.'

Sydney Banks, *The Missing Link*[10]

I've done my best to convey the essence of these principles, but any description can only go so far in capturing their pure power and potential. Think of them as a guide for your own exploration as you reflect on your life experience and the lives of others.

Universal Mind: the intelligence behind life

When your heart is beating, are you telling it to do that, or does it just happen?

When you get a cut, how does your skin know how and when to begin healing?

We experience the body's capacity to heal, often without human intervention. When my sister broke her wrist, the bone slowly mended despite the intense pain she endured for some time.

Every day, we are learning more about neuroplasticity; the brain's innate ability to constantly adapt, change and renew.

And it's not just humans that have these awe-inspiring qualities. How do birds instinctively know how to navigate to faraway places? It's as if they have a built-in GPS.

Animals can alter their appearance to attract a mate or blend into their surroundings. As well as being able to change texture and colour in the blink of an eye, an octopus can mimic other sea creatures to protect itself. And while bats can navigate complete darkness, the ever so delicate monarch butterfly can travel thousands of miles for winter.

We're also learning that, even though plants don't have a nervous system, they have memory.[11] And Japanese researchers discovered that when they put slime mould into a maze, it can find the shortest path, despite having no neurons.[12] This and other adaptive behaviour isn't fully understood yet but it demonstrates a deeper dimension of intelligence and complex problem solving that exists beyond the brain. Who knew slime could be so exciting. ☺

While none of these amazing features are under our personal control, we get a front row seat to witness the wonder and wisdom of nature, which includes you.

And in case you are wondering how the brain fits into this . . .

If the brain is like a traditional sailing boat, then *Mind* is like the wind.

Like a boat, the brain is tangible. As a physical organ located in the skull, you can see, touch and study it under a microscope. Whereas *Mind*, like the wind, is a force we cannot directly see and touch, but we feel its constant effects.

Universal Mind is one way of naming the essence of this energy or power before it takes form as any particular feature in the natural world. Different cultures and disciplines have their own names, including chi, life force, divine mind, quantum field, soul, wisdom and, if you're religious, God.

Whatever you call it, the fact that you exist is because of this energy.

> All matter is created from a formless energy that has no body of its own, until it comes into this world of time, space and matter.
>
> An important thing to realise is that Universal Mind and personal mind are not two minds thinking differently, but two ways of using the same mind.

Sydney Banks

I think I see for a moment how our minds are all threaded together — how any live mind today is of the very same stuff as Plato's and Euripides's. It is only a continuation and development of the same thing. It is this common mind that binds the whole world together; and all the world is mind.

Virginia Woolf

The over-all number of minds is just one. I venture to call it indestructible since it has a peculiar timetable, namely mind is always now. There is really no before and after for mind. There is only a now that includes memories and expectations.

Nobel Prize winner Erwin Schrödinger

Universal Thought: the power to personalise life

We were fast asleep in bed and, suddenly, my boyfriend shouted out. His body jumped, jolting me awake. 'What happened?' I asked, not expecting an answer.

'I fell off my bike.'

We laughed so hard that it took ages to fall asleep again. Damn that bike!

We exist in a world of *Thought*, like fish exist in water. While you're awake and while you sleep, you're experiencing the principle or power of *Thought*, producing emotions, sensations and perceptions, triggering neurological and physical responses.

'Thought is a divine power. It is an element that can never be broken down into smaller segments. It is we human beings that use Thought to produce such things as our feelings, moods, and our overall perceptions of life.'

Sydney Banks

Useful distinction:
Principle vs Products

You experience thousands of different personal thoughts and feelings each day. Sometimes, we have hundreds of familiar and recurring thoughts or feelings, in the form of patterns and habits. This book is exploring the Principle of *Thought* – the constant neutral power behind everything your mind creates and perceives.

Principle of *Thought*	$\rightleftharpoons$	Products of *Thought*
The fact that we can think up anything		Mental activity including feelings, perceptions, moods, emotions, states of mind, behaviour.
Formless, impersonal energy and source of all psychological experience		Personalised , subjective, unique expressions of the above.
A constant force of unlimited creative potential		Ever changing moment to moment forms of *Thought* including: opinions, ideas, beliefs, solutions, values, rules, reasons, religion, meaning, judgements, dreams, expectations, culture,, memories, morals, preferences, styles, personality, identity, assumptions, prejudice, categories, models, habits, conditioning.

Here's another visual to help make sense of this . . .

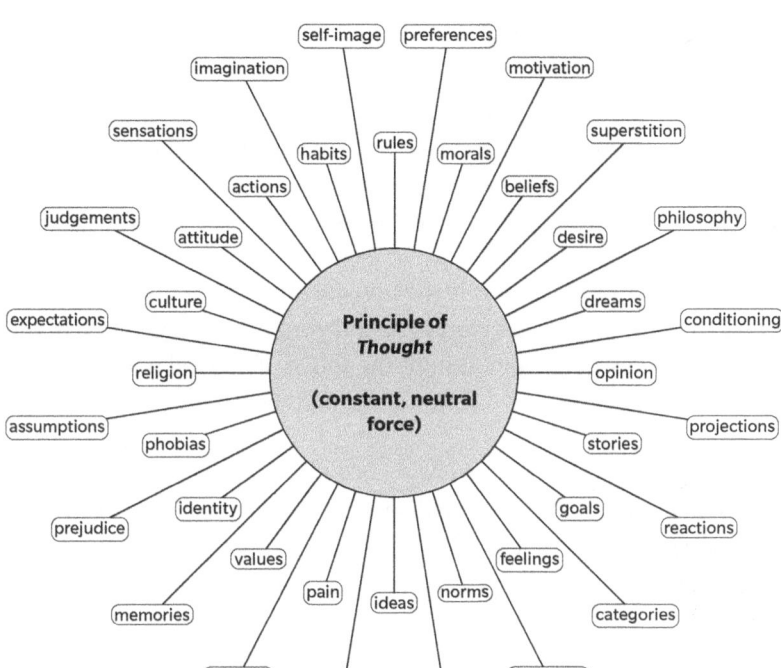

> Thought is always doing a great deal, but it tends to say that it hasn't done anything, that it is just telling you the way things are. But Thought affects everything. It has created everything we see in this building. It has affected all the trees, it has affected the mountains, the plains and the farms and the factories and scientists and technology.
>
> Thought creates the world, then says 'I didn't do it'.

Professor David Bohm, physicist and author

Universal Consciousness: the power to be aware

Have you ever found a bruise on your body and wondered how the hell it got there? I've collided with random objects and been totally oblivious. It's only later when you notice a mark that you realise it happened. But how are we able to recognise something in the first place?

The power of *Consciousness* is the invisible force that makes you aware of yourself and the world around you. It allows you to feel the warmth of the sun on your skin or the touch of a loved one. It's how you're able to recognise your thoughts, feel your feelings and listen to your instincts.

Have you ever had a sudden realisation about something you've been pondering for ages, that suddenly becomes crystal clear? That's also the power of *Consciousness* in action. It helps you connect the dots and uncover new possibilities.

But it isn't just a human feature. Birds and squirrels can remember where they hid their food. Elephants, dolphins and many other animals show emotions like grief and love. They're also great problem solvers and show complex social behaviour. And it doesn't stop there. We're learning that plants are aware of their surroundings too.

It's all thanks to this universal force that pervades every aspect of our being. And, while it's one of life's greatest mysteries, here are some powerful pointers.

> **We cannot get behind consciousness. Everything that we talk about, everything that we regard as existing, assumes Consciousness.**

Nobel Prize winner Max Planck

To have an emotion or feeling one must have Thought to create the feeling, plus Consciousness to be aware of it. I'm talking about Consciousness as a spiritual, neutral power before human experience.

Sydney Banks

Consciousness is the central fact of your life.

Without Consciousness there is nothing. The only way you experience your body and the world of mountains and people, trees and dogs, stars and music is through your subjective experiences [. . .]. You act and move, see and hear, love and hate, remember the past and imagine the future. But ultimately, you only encounter the world in all of its manifestations via Consciousness.

Neuroscientist Christof Koch

As humans, we tend to focus on the most visible, tangible parts of our reality . . . the earthly, material bits that we can see, touch, hear and feel. You get mesmerised by the movie in your mind and the sensations in your body. But how often do we stop to look behind the scenes at how the entire experience is happening in the first place?

If we use the analogy of the projector from earlier . . .

Mind is the power source that brings everything into existence. Without it there would be no movie which means no psychological reality.

Thought is the film reel. Without it there would be no 'content' (thoughts, feelings, sensations) to experience.

Consciousness is the light that turns the film into the multi-sensory subjective reality that you're experiencing right now. Without it you wouldn't be aware of any thoughts and feelings. You wouldn't be aware of existence.

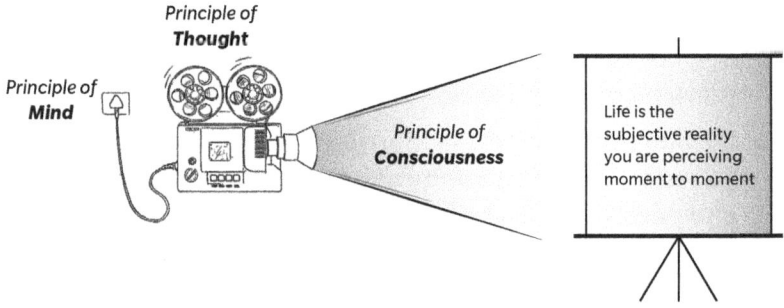

Like gravity, you can't see or touch these principles, but you're experiencing the impact of them in every moment of your life. They're the essential building blocks of your reality. Because of them, you get to experience every feeling, from the depths of despair to the deepest peace and joy. While you're awake and asleep, you revisit the past and imagine and create new futures.

My dog Eddie loves dropping his toys right on the edge of any steep bank or hill. You'll often find me scrambling down through brambles, looking for his balls ☺. Eddie hasn't quite grasped gravity, or maybe he has and the joke's on me.

You might be thinking this is all very interesting, but what's this got to do with resilience? And the answer, as I'm discovering, is *everything*. Our understanding of reality shapes every part of how we navigate life. When we misunderstand or overlook how it works it means;

More insecurity, less peace

Feeling powerless is inevitable when we think that there's a separate world 'out there' which can dictate how we think, feel and behave. This misperception traps us in cycles of insecurity, attachment and fear-based behaviour which leads to . . .

More controlling, less being

If you're attributing your feelings and actions to something beyond the power of mind, you'll inevitably feel the need to manage or control what appear to be 'external triggers'. We end up ruminating on the past, incessantly worrying about the future or trying to control situations and people so that we can feel better. And, when we can't influence those 'outer' circumstances, we try to change our feelings or behaviour using various coping strategies, all of which can lead to . . .

More mental clutter, less clarity

If there's an abundance of inner and outer factors that can affect your resilience and emotional well-being, it's easy to get caught up in overthinking, strategising or stressing about how to handle it all. Our mind becomes noisy and crowded, to the point where we can't think straight and we lose perspective.

But . . . as soon as we realign with the inside>out nature of reality, it's like a reset that helps you break free from cycles of insecurity and unhelpful patterns of behaviour.

For example, when you're not blaming others for your own feelings and behaviour, it opens the door to more understanding, compassion, honesty and trust. And when you're not feeling victimised by life, it takes a huge weight off your shoulders. You can breathe easier, gracefully navigate life's challenges, and experience each moment with more lightness, courage, and perspective.

The past and future can only exist as an experience of the principle of *Thought* taking form in each moment. When we remember this, it lands us back in the moment and changes your relationship with memories, feelings and sensations that might otherwise seem scary or overwhelming.

No matter what has happened in the past, or what may happen in the future, it cannot limit the love, peace, joy and fulfilment that you can experience in the present.

Join me in the next chapter to explore the subtractive magic that brings you back to stillness and sanity.

In essence

- ♥ We're always being guided by a deeper intelligence or wisdom behind life. Our job is to listen.
- ♥ Life/reality is being experienced from the inside>out 100% of the time, without exception.
- ♥ The principle of *Thought* is constantly being brought to life through your senses, via *Consciousness*, crafting a personal, subjective reality in each moment.
- ♥ We can use our minds more wisely and avoid unnecessary and prolonged suffering when we are aligned with the inside>out reality.
- ♥ The system behind the scenes is responsible for everything that we experience as our reality. Mind is the most powerful force in the universe.

Bonus chapter materials here: http://www.chantalburns.com/bulletproof-chapter2-the-resilience-myth/

chapter 3

How to reset and return to sanity

'The soul grows by subtraction,
not addition.'

Henry David Thoreau

In 1960, Wilma Rudolph was known as the fastest woman on earth. She broke multiple world records. An incredible achievement by anyone's standards, yet this is someone who contracted polio and scarlet fever when she was four years old. Her family were told she would never walk again. But, with determination, dedication and support, she won her first bronze Olympic medal at the age of 16.

Four years later, she became the first American woman to win three gold medals in track and field in a single Olympic Games. She was later honoured with the 'Wilma Rudolph Award of Courage' which to this day continues to celebrate female athletes who show perseverance and fortitude in the face of adversity. She said;

'Never underestimate the power of dreams and the influence of the human spirit. We are all the same in this notion: The potential for greatness lives within each of us.'

Resilience takes many forms. On 4 January 1983, Archie Williams was arrested for the rape and attempted murder of a woman in her home in Baton Rouge, Louisiana. In April of the same year, he was convicted and sentenced to life without parole in what was known to be a particularly violent prison. He was 22 years old.

Archie Williams always insisted he was innocent. At least three people confirmed he was with them that evening. There was no fingerprint match or anything linking him to the crime, apart from the testimony of the victim who picked him out of a line-up. Any evidence that might have helped him was either withheld or ignored.

After 10 years in prison, the Innocence Project took on Archie's case and got access to crucial DNA evidence that would vindicate him. But that process took over 20 years. In March 2019, after serving 37 years in prison for a crime he didn't commit, Archie Williams was exonerated. When a reporter asked how he got through it, he said, 'Freedom is of the mind. I went to prison, but I never let my mind go to prison.'

Archie's courage and enduring hope are expressions of that ordinary magic we all have within. The Innocence team's compassion and resolve to keep pursuing justice in the face of so many false starts and setbacks is also testament to the human spirit.

What inner strengths have *you* discovered during those times in your life when you've felt most up against it?

Below are some of the natural qualities most often associated with resilience, along with how to recognise them in daily life. But it's important to remember that, even though you might not always see or feel these qualities, *you came into the world with them*. They are already and always part of you.

Seven innate qualities and signs of psychological/emotional resilience

Self-efficacy	**What it is**: Backing yourself, trusting your inner resources **Some signs of self-efficacy:** • Maintaining healthy boundaries, e.g. saying no when appropriate • Asserting and expressing your needs without apology • A sense of agency, feeling empowered	**What it isn't**: Perfectionism, arrogance, being immune to failure, denial of limitations, a quality that needs external validation

➤

Tenacity	**What it is:** Determination, resolve, endurance **Some signs of tenacity:** • Setbacks don't derail your efforts or inspiration • Failure doesn't faze you – it's useful learning • Persistent and purposeful • Being focused • Knowing when to hold your ground, quit or change direction	**What it isn't:** Bull-dozing, forcing, rigid, neglectful dogmatic, coercive, tunnel-visioned
Optimism	**What it is:** Being hopeful, positive, constructive **Some signs of optimism:** • When we recognise potential and possibility • Focusing on solutions • Listening for strengths (not just negatives/weakness) • Being in touch with reality and not avoiding the 'difficult' stuff	**What it isn't:** Blind faith, delusional thinking, irrational hope, denial, forced positivity
Flexibility	**What it is:** Being agile, adaptable, responsive **Signs of flexibility include:** • Appreciating and encouraging diverse perspectives • Willingness to adapt, adjust and change course • Being open to new ideas and new ways of thinking/ behaving • Willingness to let go of ideas, opinions, rules, beliefs.	**What it isn't:** Being a doormat, trying to please everyone, indecision, lack of planning, being forced to change, compromising your boundaries, wellbeing or integrity, feeling forced to change.

Courage	**What it is:** Being brave, having guts or facing fear **Signs of courage include:** • Being honest even when it feels difficult or uncomfortable • Persevering despite feeling afraid • Inner knowing that guides your actions • Being vulnerable or taking risks • Leaning into uncertainty/ the unknown	**What it isn't:** Being reckless, ruthless, irresponsible, causing harm, hiding or suppressing feelings, not asking for help.
Empathy	**What it is:** Compassion, kindness, care for self or others **Signs of empathy include:** • Feeling moved and touched by another person's suffering • Unconditional love • Helping without feeling responsible for people's feelings or behaviour • Wanting to understand how someone thinks and feels • Respecting and acknowledging another's feelings/ emotions	**What it isn't:** Worry, fixing, guilt, attachment, agreeing, mind-reading, projecting, pity, ignoring your own needs, enabling

➤

Mental clarity	**What it is:** Mentally present, in the 'zone' or in flow	**What it isn't:** Suppressing, avoiding or numbing thoughts or feelings, absence of strong emotions, always being certain, having the answers
	Signs of mental clarity:	
	• Clear thinking • Able to focus • Creativity flows • Moving on from a thought/ feeling instead of getting stuck • Mind feels spacious • Actions are guided by wisdom, not insecurity • Able to see the funny	

Are there any qualities that you associate with being resilient, that you would love to embody more easily?

Are there any ways of being (feelings or behaviour) that you want to dial down?

If so, what do you think is getting in the way?

I used to be a professional complainer, always noticing flaws and shortcomings. It became more apparent when we were out for a meal with friends and one of them said, 'You're not going to complain, are you? I really want to come back here.'

Everyone else was nodding in agreement. 'What the hell!' I thought to myself. My ego felt bruised but a part of me knew it was warranted.

A few months later, I was out for a meal with friends and there was an issue with someone's food. One of them said, 'Go on Chantal, *you* give them feedback.' Everyone laughed, including me. 'Do it yourself. I'm not your complaints manager. I officially resign from that post!'

If we want to learn and evolve, constructive feedback is essential. When you notice and communicate what isn't working, it can spur positive change and improvement. But living in a frequent state of dissatisfaction takes you out of the moment and steals your joy.

The health benefits of gratitude have been widely publicised, and it's led to the creation of tools designed to amplify our appreciation. As an experiment several years ago, I downloaded one of many apps so I could test it out. Each day you had to post three things that you're grateful for, with the aim of experiencing positive changes in well-being and outlook.

Day 1: added a photo of my much-loved mum from a lunch together, uploaded a photo of a rose from the garden and added a few words about how much I love my work. Was filled with warm fuzzy feelings. So far, so good.

Day 2: struggled to find my third thing. How could I have so much to be thankful for, yet be unable to find just one more example? Felt irritated and closed the app.

Day 3: heard the ping reminding me to add my three things, But I was busy and it felt like an intrusion so I skipped it.

By day 5, I'd developed an allergic reaction to the notifications and, less than a week into the experiment, '3 Things' had gone to app heaven.

When I shared my experience with a friend, she told me she did a similar experiment during a difficult period in her life when she and her daughter were struggling with their mental health. Her daily practice of intentional gratitude helped her find some much-needed light during a very dark time. She couldn't speak highly enough of the whole experience.

So, why did it work for her and not for me?

This is also a common question when it comes to practices like meditation or mindfulness. Some of my friends love meditating and swear by its powerful effects while others would rather binge-watch hilarious cat videos.

Maybe it's not the tool or the practice that holds the magic. What if it's simpler than that?

Have you ever been overcome with deep feelings of contentment, appreciation or love? And have you noticed how these feelings can happen naturally and without any effort?

Michelangelo famously said, 'I saw the angel in the marble and carved until I set him free.' He believed that his job as a sculptor was simply to reveal what is already present within the raw materials. In the same way, resilient qualities are not something we have to strive for because they're already within, waiting to be uncovered.

The power of subtraction

As a footballer gets ready to take the penalty shot, the air is heavy with anticipation. It feels like the world stops, as fans collectively hold their breath. We know instinctively that the player who is in the moment, and not in their head, is more likely to score while those who hesitate or overthink are more likely to miss.

Andy Murray, one of the world's best tennis players, discovered this for himself and began to put his inner game first. Despite recurring injury and several surgeries, he went on to win major tournaments, defying the odds.

World champion golfer Rory McIlroy said, 'It's funny how the mind works, where when it doesn't go right you know every single little detail, but when it does go right, you can't really put your finger on why. It's this psychological phenomenon that it's just sort of being in the flow state and you're not really thinking that much . . . '[1]

That flow state or being in the zone, is the experience of just being.

'When we are in flow, we are fully present, totally engaged, and at one with the task at hand. We lose track of time and self, and the world seems to fade away.'

Steven Kotler, author

Have you ever missed a junction on the motorway because your mind was on something else? Maybe you know people who are always losing their keys (or similar) because they're distracted when they put them down? Ever pressed send on a text message when you didn't mean to? Or put your underwear in the fridge instead of the washing machine? OK, maybe that's just me.

A distracted or busy mind becomes so normal that we don't even notice there's another way to be.

Thought experiment
Catch

- -

To try this out, you need a tennis ball or any small ball with clear markings that you can see from a distance.

You're going to ask someone to throw the tennis ball to you as if you're playing catch. Make it as challenging as you can either in terms of speed or distance.

Play 1: As they make the first few throws, think about how crucial it is that you catch the ball . . . how you must not miss. Think about your ability to catch the ball and whether you will manage it or not.

Now you're going to shift your awareness.

Play 2: For the next few catches, simply put your attention on the ball as it comes towards you, as you watch the direction the ball is spinning.

When you've done that a few times, reflect on the difference between play 1 and play 2. How did the experience differ?

- -

Most people say that they catch the ball easily when they're just watching the spin and not thinking about anything else. The first time I tried this, I was surprised at how the ball seemed to land in my hands without any effort on my part.

This experiment helps to highlight the difference between thinking about an experience versus being *in* the experience. And this distinction applies to every aspect of our lives, even chronic pain.

I've struggled with migraine throughout my life. Sometimes, the pain's been so extreme that I've felt suicidal. During a particularly severe episode a few years ago, for the first time ever I noticed the chatter in my head. 'Why does this keep happening to me?' 'Omg, it hurts so much.' 'I need to sleep but how can I sleep with all this pain?'.

And then something occurred to me. 'What would the migraine be like without judging and resenting it?' As I lay there, I was able to tune into the feelings and sensations. And each time I heard myself judging, complaining or resisting, I would bring my attention back to the sheer sensations. I could feel myself begin to relax, just a little. I continued to tune in and shift my attention to the present moment. Eventually, I fell into a deep sleep.

Until that day, I'd always considered migraine as purely physical and biological. But I've come to understand that it's psychological and neurological in nature. Pain is perception and sensations are the raw ingredients.

I've heard people talk about the difference between physical and emotional suffering but it wasn't until that moment, mid-migraine, when I realised what this means. And I finally understood what Alan Watts meant when he said;

'Can you, at the same time read this sentence and think about yourself reading it? You will find that, to think about yourself reading it, you must for a brief second stop reading. The first experience is reading. The second experience is the thought "I am reading".'

Alan Watts, *The Wisdom of Insecurity*[2]

I was having painful sensations and I was also judging them non-stop. I'd never noticed, until that moment, that much of my suffering was coming from my own commentary . . . my judgements, resistance, self-pity, worry, etc.

When you recognise mental noise for what it is, that moment of recognition is like pressing reset. The mind naturally quiets or settles, bringing you back to the moment . . . back to stillness.

Useful distinction:
addition vs subtraction

Leidy Klotz wrote a book called *Subtract*.[3] He tells a story about playing Lego with his young son Ezra. They were trying to fix a bridge that was unstable. Klotz turned to grab another block and, by the time he turned back, his son had removed one, and the bridge was now level.

We tend to overlook the power of subtraction in all areas of life. When it comes to a healthy mind, we reach for more information, more strategies and tools so we can feel less anxious, or be calmer, more confident, etc.

But true resilience is the removal of outside<in interference that creates mental noise and stops you from experiencing the ordinary magic (innate qualities) you were born with.

So, how does mental noise get created?

The *when-then* thought trap

From an early age, we're bombarded with messages that happiness and well-being come from what we own, how we look, how others treat us, how much money we have, or whether we have kids. The list goes on.

We get teased with the promise of inner peace once we've got the latest gadget, the perfect pout, the luxury car. But all we get is a short-term high from a hit of oxytocin. And that fleeting sense of satisfaction soon dissolves.

We think our worth is wedded to other people's approval so we end up vying for validation, giving away our power and losing sight of what's already within.

Here are some common *when-thens*:

When I get my dream job, *then* I'll be fulfilled.

When I have children, *then* I'll be complete.

When I find my perfect partner, *then* I'll be truly happy.

When I feel more confident, *then* I'll go for that promotion.

When I don't get enough 'likes', *then* I feel insecure.

When I retire, *then* I can finally do the things that I love.

When I win the lottery, *then* I will be secure/content.

What are some of your *when-thens*?

. . . .

. . . .

Have you noticed that, even when you get the *whens*, you don't always experience the *thens*?!

Jon has a lot of material wealth and success and he's never happy or satisfied. There's always something else, something better that will make him more content. 'My dissatisfaction drives me to get better results but, when I get them, I'm still not content. I just want some peace,' he says during a session.

I can relate to Jon's story. I used to think that if I felt content, I might lose my mojo. Turns out that's not true.

And for every person that believes having children will complete them, there are many who feel they or their lives are no less complete without children of their own.

This doesn't deny or diminish the deep sense of longing that some of us will experience, but it's empowering to know that longing and not longing are created the same way.

We attach our peace of mind (or lack of) to things that have no power to affect our feelings and behaviour. And this false dependency creates feelings that seem to reinforce this false perception.

We're led to believe that our worth or contentment comes from material success, so we drive ourselves into the ground grasping for an unreachable horizon.

As film maker Michael Shaw describes in one of his newsletters, we are living in 'a culture hooked on achievement, "progress" and a shallow, status related happiness'.[4]

The illusion of 'when-then' seduces our senses. We get hooked on having more and more, or better, instead of appreciating sufficiency. We've forgotten what 'enough' is.

And we can see this play out on a bigger scale in western society with over-consumption and waste. We've been taking more and more from the earth to feed our insatiable desires. This means our ecological footprint is now exceeding the planet's capacity to support our demands. Could a shift in consciousness be the answer?

There's an old story about a fisherman who offers to take a tourist for a boat ride to enjoy the island. They strike up a conversation and the tourist asks his host why he isn't out catching more fish.

The fisherman explains that he's caught enough food this month to feed his family and sell on a few at the local market. 'But you could be more successful and make more money by working longer hours and catching more fish,' he tells him.

'Why would I want that?' the fisherman asks. 'Well, then you can buy a larger boat and hire people to work for you,' the tourist replies.

'And then what?' the fisherman asks. 'Well, then you can grow your business, make more money, and eventually retire and just enjoy your life.' The fisherman looks at him and smiles, 'Ah, but I am enjoying my life.'

> **'We're misinterpreting the content of our perceptual experiences.'**
>
> **Prof. Donald D. Hoffman,**
> **neuroscientist, author[5]**

You experience an inner spiritual, psychological world of perception, sensations and emotions. And you also experience what seems to be an objectively external, separate world of stuff that you can see, hear, feel and touch. It might seem like this outer world can dictate your inner state of being. But they are one and any division can only exist in *Thought*.

It would be like believing that the roots of a tree are separate from the branches and bough when really, what is above is a reflection of what is below.

And just as the health of a tree depends on healthy roots and soil, we also need to nourish the soil of our spiritual / psychological life. Removing unnecessary division, misperception and mental noise is an essential part of that.

The Tree of Life

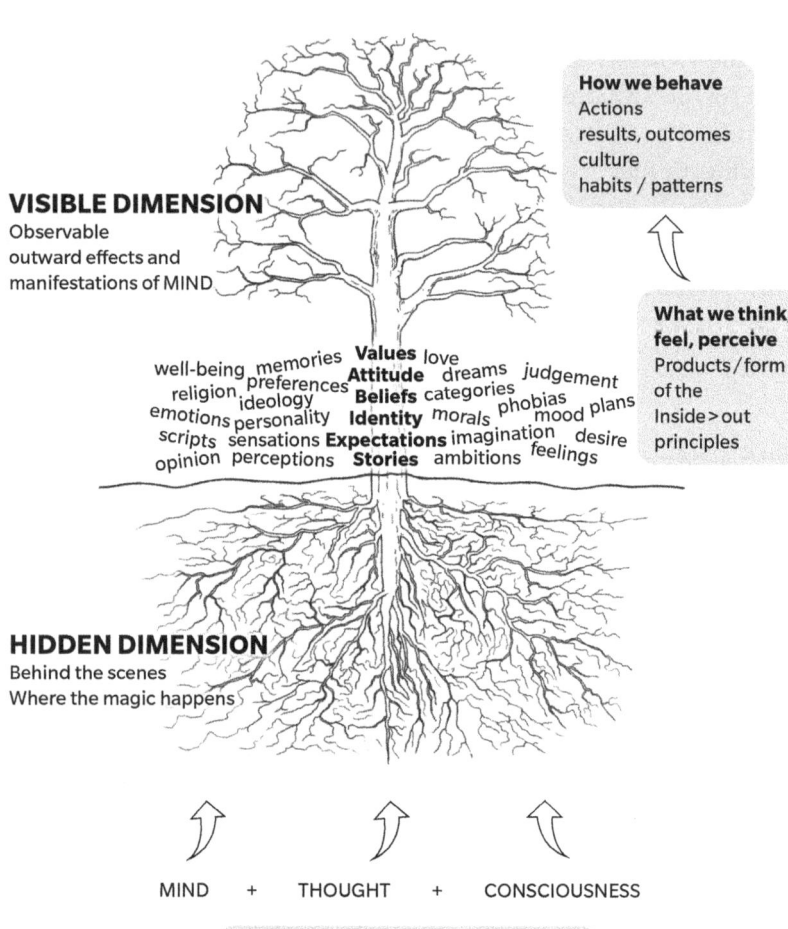

VISIBLE DIMENSION
Observable
outward effects and
manifestations of MIND

How we behave
Actions
results, outcomes
culture
habits / patterns

**What we think,
feel, perceive**
Products / form
of the
Inside > out
principles

well-being memories **Values** love
Attitude dreams judgement
religion preferences **Beliefs** categories
ideology phobias
emotions personality **Identity** morals mood plans
scripts sensations **Expectations** imagination desire
opinion perceptions **Stories** ambitions feelings

HIDDEN DIMENSION
Behind the scenes
Where the magic happens

MIND   +   THOUGHT   +   CONSCIOUSNESS

**Universal principles / Laws of nature /
Spiritual energy behind life**

The impersonal creative force behind our
personal realities–all thinking, feelings,
sensations, perceptions, attitude,
behaviour.

We live in cause–effect model of reality where we place conditions on our resilience and mental well-being which means we are always either chasing something that has no power or blaming what we believe are causes of our discontent or distress. This disempowers and disconnects us from ourselves and the world around us.

Here's a simple way to think about this.

Useful distinction:
inside-out vs outside-in

 Outside<in illusion Believing that reality works a way that it cannot.	 Inside>out reality How the mind works to create our perceptual reality.
When our thinking is at odds with the logic of how we experience reality.	How we perceive and experience reality from birth to death.
We attach our emotions, sensations, perceptions and behaviour to something *other* than the Inside>out principles of *Mind, Thought* and *Consciousness*. Our spiritual, psychological and physical reality gets split into separate inner and outer worlds and into infinite categories of experience.	Our entire felt experience (emotions sensations, perceptions, behaviour) is a product of the power of the Inside>out principles, 100% of the time. Our spiritual, psychological and physical reality is one and cannot be split into separate worlds and categories except in our mind.[6]

When we forget that reality is an inside job (which for me happens on a *daily* basis), it creates mental disturbance, manifesting in all kinds of feeling states and behaviour that include:

Emotional insecurity: fear of rejection, a sense of inadequacy, sensitivity to criticism are some of the symptoms of the outside<in illusion.

Self-consciousness: fear of being judged, being preoccupied with how others perceive us or obsession with self-image takes us out of the moment and creates more mental interference and suffering.

Anxiety and overwhelm: happens when we feel at the mercy of life and when we're trying to meet our own and other people's made-up expectations.

Resentment and hatred: holding onto ill-feeling towards ourselves or others fosters further disconnection and polarisation instead of unity, understanding or compassion.

Deflection or denial: fear can drive us to deny or distort reality, preventing us from acknowledging what is. This keeps us stuck or stops us from healing and moving forward.

Arrogance and superiority: is a result of losing sight of our shared humanity and humility because we think we know all there is to know. Insecurity is often masked by arrogance. It leads to lack of empathy, judgement, alienation, conflict, inability to grow/learn.

Perfectionism: is characterised by feeling compelled to meet some standard/level that we or someone else has made up, so that we can feel worthy, accepted, loved or enough.

Greed: gets created when we perceive a void or unwarranted feelings of lack. We then do what makes sense in the moment satisfy this unquenchable insecurity, which includes lots of 'more'. More achievement, more stuff, more power, more money. But in the outside-in illusion there will never be 'enough'.

Helplessness and despair: if we think our emotional state or our lives in general are controlled by external forces, it leads to a sense of powerlessness and dependency. We might lose sight of our innate wisdom, agency and resilience.

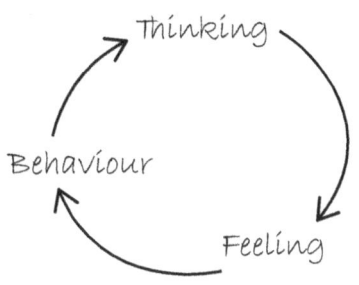

Temporary states of mind act like a lens, shaping and colouring how we think, feel and behave.

The 'thinking–feeling–behaviour' cycle becomes a self-reinforcing feedback loop.

When Jane is in a social setting, she often feels self-conscious and worries about what people think of her. As a result, she can't be herself and relax. The more insecure she gets, the more real her anxieties feel. She then tries to manage those feelings. Instead of enjoying herself and connecting with people, she tries to blend into the background and make herself invisible. It's not long before she makes her excuses and quietly leaves.

Much of the mind's activity is driven by habits of thinking, based on the past. Habits and patterns are harder to spot because they're so ingrained that they feel 'normal'. As a result, we might not stop to question the way we see the world. Instead, we justify our attitudes or behaviour with 'this is the way it is' or 'this is just the way I am'.

But normal is not the same as natural. Normal is a learned way of being. Natural is innate and universal. For example, eating three meals a day at specific times is a pattern that's considered the norm in some cultures. Natural is the feeling of hunger, and the desire to eat when hungry, both of which are innate survival mechanisms.

So how do you quiet this mental noise, break free of unhelpful patterns, and reset your resilience when you most need it?

The answer is surprisingly simple but not always easy! To reset, we need to remove misunderstanding and mythology.

'If you know something is not possible, it is a lot less tempting to believe in than if you think it is possible.'

Valda Monroe[7]

If you think the world is flat, you might be scared to venture too far in case you fall off the edge.

But when you know this isn't true, any associated fear of the 'edge' is automatically removed and you feel empowered to keep exploring.

In the same way, when you recognise outside-in noise for what it is (an illusion), any fear of falling off a psychological edge is also removed returning you back to wisdom and sanity.

In Part 2, we'll debunk the most deceptive myths and mental traps, making it much easier for you to reset and return to a free mind.

In essence

- -

♥ Resilience isn't an achievement. It is not something to strive for. Resilience is the essence of who you are.

♥ This means that all the essential qualities of resilience are already within.

♥ Mental noise caused by the outside<in illusion is what gets in the way of experiencing our innate qualities and common sense.

♥ The subtraction of outside<in thinking removes the noise, settles your mind and opens your heart.

♥ Our natural capacity to realise, recognise and become aware. . . this is how *Consciousness* shows us what we most need to learn and understand.

Bonus chapter materials here: http://www.chantalburns.com/bulletproof-chapter-3-reset/

part 2

—

Uncover resilience by removing interference

chapter 4

———

Why positive thinking is outdated

'One is a great deal less anxious if one feels perfectly free to be anxious.'

Alan Watts

It was 2013 and I was in Tokyo leading a series of inside>out coaching programmes. The positive thinking movement was gaining momentum. Many of the students told me they had been encouraging their clients to replace negative thoughts with positive ones. 'It's important to have a positive mindset,' one told me.

I shared the following story with them.

A farmer had a horse that helped his family earn a living. One day, the horse ran off. His neighbours cried out, 'Your horse ran away, what terrible luck!' The farmer replied, 'Maybe.' A few days later, the horse returned home with a bunch of wild mares. The neighbours looked in, 'Your horse is home with six new friends. What wonderful luck!' The farmer replied, 'Maybe.'

Later that week, the farmer's son was taming one of the mares, and was thrown to the ground, breaking his leg. A local villager said, 'Your son has broken his leg, what terrible luck!' The farmer replied, 'Maybe.' Then, a few weeks later, soldiers from the national army marched through the village, recruiting local lads. They couldn't take the farmer's son who was still recovering from his injury. Their friends said, 'your boy has been spared, what fantastic luck!' to which the farmer replied, 'Maybe.'

Positively deluded

I used to believe there were good and bad emotions. I strived to always think positively, whatever the situation.

The image below represents this outdated 'positive/negative' model. There are infinite flavours of feelings and emotions, so this is just a selection to illustrate the point.

Ladder of emotions

positive/high state of mind ☺	joyful, peaceful, content
	calm, grateful, compassionate
	passionate, inspired, in awe
	happy, upbeat, confident
	serene, loving, satisfied
	hopeful, optimistic
	excited, inspired, amused
	bored, critical
	discouraged, disappointed
	critical, pessimistic
	hurt, upset
	frustrated, irritated, guilty
	jealous, resentful, distressed
	worried, stressed, overwhelmed
	sad, ashamed, anxious
	embarrassed, disgusted
negative/low state of mind ☹	angry, scared, insecure
	depressed, hopeless

This model implies that:

- Feelings and emotions are fundamentally good, bad, right or wrong
- Positive (high) thoughts /feelings = resilience/thriving
- Negative (low) thoughts/feelings = lack of resilience/not thriving

Based on this, we should avoid 'negative' or undesirable feelings and emotions, in favour of positive ones.

It also implies that we need to be at the top of this imaginary ladder if we want to feel secure and resilient, and avoid the lower rungs.

It's no surprise that we end up feeling bad about feeling sad or feeling guilty about being happy. Denying, avoiding or numbing our feelings is a useful strategy if feelings are a problem that we have to fix. And, when it also seems like there's an endless list of things to blame or rely on for your state of mind, this gives us even more to think about.

Based on this outside<in model, if you want to mentally reset, there are two main options. You can either try and change your thoughts or feelings. Or you can try to manage or manipulate the situations that you think are responsible for your thoughts and feelings, e.g. other people, events, past, future, etc.

This is what we're taught and encouraged to do. And it makes total sense if we lived in an outside<in world, but we don't. And that's why so many of our attempts to feel better only make things worse or, at the very least, keeps things as they are.

When I met Lauren in 2005 through a mutual friend, she'd experienced emotional abuse by a previous boss. It was reported and all necessary legal and practical steps were taken. A year later, she was still feeling troubled and struggling to move on, so she asked for some sessions with me. In one of our conversations, I used a reframing technique where I invited her to explore some alternative perspectives. The aim was to help her come to peace with the past.

After a few minutes, she said, 'It doesn't matter how many ways I think about this, I can't force myself to feel OK. It's like I am trying to convince myself to believe something that isn't true, as if my feelings aren't valid.'

As Lauren re-hashed her memories of what happened, she felt the hurt and upset as if it was happening to her again in that very moment. Her face reddened. Her voice was trembling. She got more animated. I watched her being sucked back into the past, into emotional quicksand, and I wasn't sure how to help her out. Her increasing upset only seemed to reinforce and prolong her suffering.

Monsters under the bed

Imagine a young child wakes up crying in the night uncontrollably because they believe there's a one-eyed monster under the bed. To console them, you have three options.

The first option is to bring them into your bed. This does nothing to address the cause but it makes a short-term difference because they immediately go to sleep.

The second option is to soothe their upset by saying, 'It's OK, don't worry, the monster is friendly and means no harm.' This approach might settle them down in the short term, but it also maintains a false belief in one-eyed monsters.

The third option is to peer under the bed together, so they can see for themselves that it's not real.

The following is a useful way to think about the dynamics of change. I want to make a distinction between short term, 'more of the same' kind of change versus deep and lasting transformation.

Levels of change[1]

You can think of change as having three fundamental levels ranging from shallow through to transformative. Let's use an example related to increasing mental wellbeing.

First Order Change: minor modifications

We try some relaxation techniques or meditation for 10 minutes every day. We go to bed earlier. We try to improve our diet. We start doing yoga once a week. We do some journaling. Maybe we avoid situations.

It's a change to our usual routine and might bring short term relief but doesn't address the core issue.

While we've made some adjustments, our world view hasn't changed. It's like tweaking the settings on your device but the software and overall system remains the same.

Second Order Change: significant but reversible

We delve into our thinking. This might involve deeper therapeutic techniques. It might include Cognitive Behavioral Therapy. Perhaps we examine core beliefs and try to change them. We

➤

revisit events from the past. We practice self-compassion or self-acceptance. We look at patterns of behaviour. Or we put a positive spin on the situation, to try and shift how we feel about it. We try new coping strategies.

There is more potential here for sustained relief or long-term improvement, but it tends to be an 'issue by issue' approach rather than wholesale change. This is like a software update.

Third Order Change – Transformative, irreversible

This is the deepest dimension of change. It involves a radical, wholesale shift in perspective or worldview that fundamentally transforms the way we see and interact with ourselves, others, and the world around us.

It's like discovering the world isn't flat. Once you see it, you cannot unsee it.

This change goes beyond beliefs and beyond all personal ideas or concepts. It gets to the underlying nature of reality. For example, we realise that stress is not an inherent feature of the world, but rather a product of the mind's tendency to create a sense of separateness and insecurity.

This level of change goes beyond software updates eg. changing your thinking. It is a complete system reset by transforming how you think *Thought* and reality works.

The following figure illustrates this distinction.

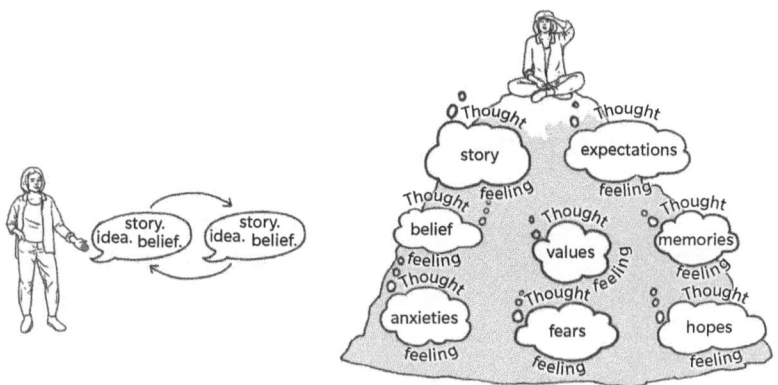

Managing thoughts/feelings	vs	Understand the nature of reality
Focus: Actively attempting to control, alter, or manipulate thinking, feelings, or behaviour.		**Focus:** Zoom out to understand the creative process behind all thoughts, feelings and behaviour.
Involves: Techniques including belief change, reframing, positive thinking, affirmations, analysing the past, and other strategies aimed at modifying individual thoughts, emotions or behaviour in desired direction.		**Involves:** Exploring the psycho-spiritual nature of resilience and the implications/benefits of a deeper awareness of how the principle of *Thought* works.

Lauren had a monster under the bed and I was trying to help her change how she was thinking about it so she could be free of the past. But I came to realise that it wasn't her thinking or emotions that were preventing her from moving on. And it wasn't the past either. It never is. I had the wrong target.

What neither of us understood was that:

⇨ Past events have no power over you and cannot hurt you in the present.

⇨ The past can only exist as an experience of the power of *Thought* passing through your consciousness *now* in the form of memories, creating feelings and sensations that come and go in each moment.

This is the conversation we needed to have . . . to zoom out, and like the woman at the top of the hill, explore the human experience from a higher vantage point.

Why feelings are like fruit

Fruit varies in form, colour, taste and texture. Some we like and others we avoid yet, at their core, they're all fruit.

Similarly, we experience a variety of feelings and emotions that we judge, embrace or avoid.

Despite their apparent differences, they all originate from the same universal, neutral power of *Thought*.

Beyond positive and negative

When we judge and label our thoughts or feelings as good or bad, positive or negative, we are mentally splitting the Principle of *Thought* into categories or segments. It's like saying there is good and bad gravity. But all feelings and emotions from the most inspiring and ecstatic, to the darkest, most depressing, is the same energy of life moving through us.

'There are no components to Thought. Thought is a divine power. It is an element that can never be broken down into smaller segments."

Sydney Banks, The Missing Link

It's how we relate to our feelings that matters. Guilt often gets a bad name but it can wake us up to what matters. It might nudge you to apologise or re-evaluate something in your life. And it can also create self judgement and suffering.

A knife isn't good or bad. It can be used to hurt someone or it can be used to prise open a pickle jar or cut your carrots. The knife itself is neutral.

It's the same with feelings, they are neutral energy and it's what we do with that energy that matters.

"But let me tell you about anger. Anger is a beautiful necessary catalyst for change. But anger needs to ignite something. It's a terrible lifetime companion.'

'When we see something that is unfair, unjust, lacks equity, our response of anger is what fuels change. But to stay in it perpetually, there's a lot of physical, emotional and spiritual costs.'

Brené Brown[2]

Yes but . . . surely if I think more positively, things are more likely to work out.

The 'Law of Attraction' became popular in the early 1990s and is based on the belief that what/how you think determines what you attract into your life. For example, if you think negatively, bad things are more likely to happen and if you think positively, you'll transmit higher vibrations into the world and this will manifest better results.

Our well-intentioned preoccupation with positivity can lead to denial and pretence. Like we touched on earlier, there's a fine line between being positive and being deluded.

A delusion is positive thinking that's misaligned with reality. It's the equivalent of sticking your head in the sand and hoping it will all be better soon. Whereas true resilience is about being firmly in reality without sugar coating or avoiding it.

Positive thinking does not equal clarity and perspective

'If merely "feeling good" could decide, drunkenness would be the supremely valid human experience.'[3]

William James, 1902

I've always believed that being optimistic and finding the positives in a situation is the best way to live. I've also learned that using your personal feelings to guide action, can lull you into a false sense of security and poor judgement.

Useful distinction:
positive/negative vs credible/clear

The 'positive/negative' belief system implies that we can't make wise decisions if we are feeling sad or upset as these 'negative' emotions might somehow cloud our clarity.

Vivienne, a friend and colleague, was reflecting on this in relation to her divorce. As they discussed ending their marriage, she often felt sad, guilty or regretful. Despite these feelings, she knew deep down that it was the right thing to do, so they went ahead.

If she had used her personal feelings as a guide, the guilt or sadness might have stopped her from making that change. Years down the line, she's able to look back and recognise how important it is to be guided by what's right, rather than what does or doesn't *feel good* in the moment.

Two of my clients recently told me that they make some of their worst decisions when they are overly excited. Positivity can lull us into a false sense of sanity. We can get carried away with ourselves. Insideout isn't about being in a particular state of mind.

Imagine that you're in a positive mood and you attribute those feelings to a beautiful sunset or to the person next to you. That would be a delusion – a lovely one, but still a delusion.

'Doesn't it take the joy out of sunsets and rainbows if you know they aren't actually making you feel good?' my friend asked me. I shared this quote with her from Carl Sagan:[4]

> **'It does no harm to the romance of the sunset to know a little about it.'**

The truth is, I'm more in awe of everything, including the fact that all our feelings, from the lovely deep ones to the crappy, horrible ones, are all being created within our own consciousness. That's pretty incredible when you think about it.

I get moved and inspired more easily now because I'm not scared to feel. When I watch a movie, I get really immersed, often shouting at the characters 'Nooooo, what are you doing?!' or crying my eyes out, much to my partner's irritation. Although, I guess you probably shouldn't do that at the cinema.

It was during a phone call with a friend that I noticed things had changed. As normal, she asked how I was. 'Yeah, I'm fine, a bit low today but OK. How about you?' I replied. 'Why are you down?' she asked.

Typically, I would have jumped headlong into a discussion about how I felt, why I felt that way, etc. I would have analysed and dissected and tried to work it all out. But this time was different. I knew it was just a low mood and I didn't need to fix it or change how I was feeling. And that was very different to before.

A client once said that managing her feelings was like a second job that she wasn't getting paid for. I can relate. But the thing is, you're designed to feel all the feels. And it's much easier to handle setbacks or disappointments when we're not fighting our feelings or afraid to feel them. Instead, you can just let them come and go as they're designed to.

But don't get me wrong. I still need to talk things through and share my feelings sometimes. The difference now is that I know my emotions (or anyone else's) are not something that need to be fixed or changed because the feelings themselves aren't a problem when we understand what they are made of.

Here's another popular idea that keeps us stuck.

The myth of choosing

You've probably heard people say things like *'Happiness is a choice'*, *'Don't be a Debbie Downer'* or *'Smile, it could be worse'*, and you think to yourself, 'It will be worse when I've punched you on the nose.'

OK, just me then.

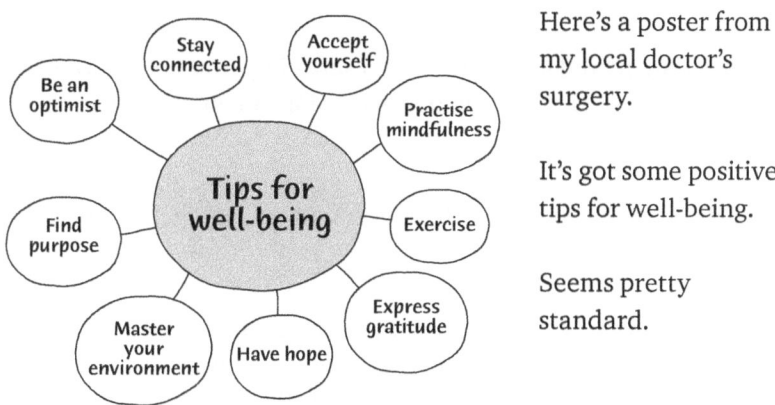

Here's a poster from my local doctor's surgery.

It's got some positive tips for well-being.

Seems pretty standard.

But telling someone to have hope when they're in a deeply depressed state is like asking someone in a dark room to just 'see' without providing a source of light. It's the same if we expect someone to exercise when they can barely drag themselves out of bed.

It's not that we don't know what's good for us. We know that having enough quality sleep is beneficial, that eating nutritious food is better than stuffing ourselves full of sugar, or that smoking 100 cigarettes a day is bad for our lungs. We also know that dwelling in a depressed state of mind is horrible. But the idea that we can just choose to be happy or choose not to feel something, isn't true.

If it worked that way, we wouldn't have a mental health crisis and relationships would be mostly harmonious. If I could, I would choose to feel more grateful, compassionate, or peaceful on demand. But as powerful as we are, we don't get to pick emotions from an a la carte mood menu.

Here's what happens. Instead of choosing, you get a new thought, a moment of clarity. You realise what's keeping you stuck. And that old belief, story or script that's been running in the background of your mind gets deleted. But this process happens so fast, that it seems as if we can just choose to be happy or choose not to be distressed.

Being told to feel a different way when you're in the depths of despair, can invalidate emotions and suffering. And not just that. Feelings play a crucial role in our lives. More about this in the next chapter.

So while we can't summon a feeling at will, we *can* invite particular ways of being.

You see the difference? One says, I can control being, let's say, compassionate. The other is saying, I care about and want to invite more compassion into my life. And this helps to direct our consciousness in a particular direction.

Given how powerful and deceptive the mind is, we need a more reliable way to navigate our emotional life. During a seminar in Tokyo, one of the students Hikari shared her insight.

'I thought I had to always be happy or put a positive spin on everything. But it's not about that. It's not about positivity or negativity. It's about perspective.'

Wait, whaaat?! This hit me like a ton of bricks. I had been promoting positive thinking without realising it. Hikari saw something that was rooted in truth.

Resilience is not about positive or negative. It's about whether we are aligned with reality or not.

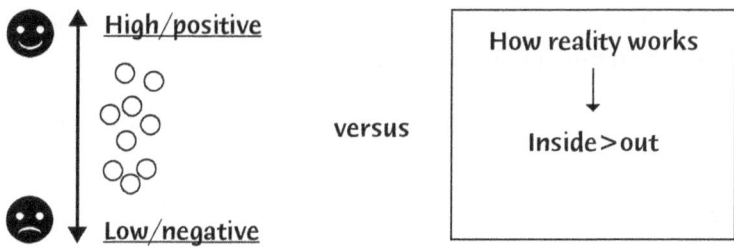

How you are feeling in any moment is not an indicator of how resilient you are at your essence. These two things are not connected, except in our heads.

Resilience is a universal, spiritual, ever-present quality that exists independent of your ever-changing personal thoughts and feelings.

Instead of focusing on *what* you are thinking or feeling, come back to *where* those feelings and sensations are really coming from. What is their true nature?

In the next chapter, we'll explore how reality works when it comes to anxiety, stress or burnout.

In essence

- -

♥ A changing state of mind is not an indicator of how resilient you are – it's an indicator of the mind's activity in each moment.

♥ There are no 'good' or 'bad' feelings. All feelings are created via the power of Thought, which means . . .

♥ We don't need to fix feelings. We just need to understand them as being the nature of human experience.

♥ Emotions are energy taking form in the mind and body. They come and go like clouds in the sky.

♥ Resilience is a constant spiritual quality that can never be taken from you. Like sky behind clouds, resilience is always here.

♥ Courage, compassion and clarity is not about being more positive or less negative. It's about feeling all the feels, being aligned with reality, and having perspective.

Bonus chapter materials here: http://www.chantalburns.com/bulletproof-chapter-4-why-positive-thinking-is-outdated/

chapter 5

Freedom from stress, anxiety and burnout

'The mind is its own place, and in
itself can make a heaven of hell and
a hell of heaven.'

John Milton

'I decided the only sensible thing to do was go to the doctor. I literally couldn't see how I could do another day . . . '

For Zoe, this was the beginning of burnout, an experience shared by millions across the UK and globally. The World Health Organisation recognised burnout as being caused by chronic workplace stress, which they described as the 'health epidemic of the twenty-first century'.[1]

At the time of writing this, stress, anxiety or depression accounts for around half of all work-related ill health and 55% of sick days in the UK.[2] In our own 'State of Mind' study, *'stress, anxiety and worry'* was the top-rated reason for underperforming at work. Anxiety is also reportedly the most common mental 'disorder' in the USA, affecting 40 million adults.[3]

Here's Zoe talking about what happened when she saw her doctor.

'I remember vividly having the conversation with her and saying that I didn't want to be signed off with work-related stress. I wanted to put something else in the sick note so I said to her, please just sign me off with IBS. I'd rather be signed off with IBS than for someone to think I had mental health issues. I can laugh now, but at the time there was a great stigma surrounding mental health. I remember senior managers saying to me that if someone's had stress, they're never really 100% after that . . . that you can never fully rely on them . . . that they could never deal with work pressure again. So that was very much in the back of my mind when I was sitting in front of the GP asking her to sign this sick note.'

That was several years ago and since then many high-profile people are speaking out about their mental health and there are lots of podcasts, books and other products which help to make it less taboo. But in some parts of society, it's almost the opposite. Mental health is being glorified,[4] with young people talking about taking medication as if they're sweets. In the UK, anti-depressants for 5–12-year-olds has increased by 41%.[5]

It's important to normalise mental health but not to the degree that psychiatric drugs are being glamorised on social media. For example, influencers have been sharing Prozac-shaped pillows that can be purchased online.

What are we missing and how can we prevent needless suffering for those that we love and care about?

'. . . the seeing of an untruth is the biggest element in its undoing.'

Adyashanti[6]

In the moment that old ideas collapse, so does their influence, and that's when you find your freedom. So, let's collapse some old ideas about stress and anxiety.

It's true that we're born with an incredible survival system. When we're in danger, the 'fight or flight' response springs into action, supercharging our senses and sharpening reactions by triggering biological, hormonal changes that bring the focus and energy you need in that moment. This marvel is another testament to the resilience in Mother Nature's design.

Veteran psychiatrist of forty-plus years, Dr Bill Pettit MD, elaborates on this survival mechanism during an interview with friend and author Jamie Smart.[7]

'It's designed to save resources like a programme shutting down to allow another programme to run. That system allows us to run through a fire and not feel the pain until we have left the building.'

While this safety system is meant to last a matter of minutes, many of us are living on high alert for several hours a day or even days and weeks at a time. That's because we're sounding the stress alarm not just for genuine danger, but when our ego or sense of self feels threatened. And, for many of us, this happens on a daily or even an hourly basis.

Prolonged periods in high alert lead to symptoms including high blood pressure, anxiety, insomnia, eczema, IBS, brain fog, loss of appetite or over-eating. Chronic stress triggers panic attacks and can lead to depression or heart disease, compromising our immune system.

Seventy six per cent of respondents from our study said anxiety and worry has a negative impact on their work-life, including patience, clarity of thinking, energy, motivation, relationships and self-confidence.

There's no doubt that the mental and physical impact of chronic stress and anxiety can be devastating. In Zoe's case, she was thrown into survival mode, 'I just became incapacitated . . . everything was too difficult. I didn't leave the house. I didn't speak to people. Going to the supermarket was just too much. I could barely leave my bed.'

Take a moment

1 How has stress, anxiety, worry or overwhelm affected your health
   and well-being?
   *For example, does it impact your sleep, diet or energy levels? Do you
   neglect self-care, for example, by overeating or under-eating? Do you
   sleep too much or not enough?*

2 How does stress, anxiety or worry manifest physically, in your
   body? What are some early signs and where do you typically
   notice it?
   *For example, some people get tense or tight in their muscles, some get
   stomach upset or other symptoms.*

3 What are some of the ways that worry, stress, anxiety or
   overwhelm has impacted your relationships, your home life,
   or your work?
   *For example, are you more detached and less present? Do you
   withdraw from people? Do you tend to lose your temper or take
   things personally? Do you ruminate and dwell on things?*

4 What coping strategies have you used to manage stress or
   anxiety?
   *Do you speak to others or do you tend to isolate yourself? Do you
   turn to substances like drugs, food or alcohol to numb or change
   how you feel? Or maybe you use exercise, meditation and other
   practices to bring some relief?*

5 If you have people in your life who are struggling with stress or
   anxiety, what patterns or behaviour have you noticed in them?

This chapter isn't about how to stop feelings of anxiety or stress
because we can't control what we think and feel any more than
we can control the direction of the wind. But as we touched on
earlier, what matters is how you relate to those feelings and to
circumstances.

When Phil's boss schedules a meeting, his imagination goes into overdrive, second guessing the reason. He loses focus for the rest of the morning. Mel agrees to give a speech at a local community event. As the date gets closer, she starts feeling anxious. She begins to doubt herself and is tempted to back out.

Jo is waiting for test results from a recent health screening. She feels constantly on edge and says she can't relax until she knows more. Alison sees a social media post about a virus making the rounds. Even though she has no symptoms, she starts obsessing about her health. Intense feelings of anxiety push her to cancel her plans. Then there's Jake. He's ruminating about a recent chat with his Dad that didn't go as well as he wanted. Feelings of unease creep into his interactions. He becomes short tempered, unable to enjoy the weekend with his kids.

How many times have you heard people complain about the stress of parenting, or finances, or juggling work and home life? How often do you hear people say they feel overwhelmed because they have too much going on, or that a future event is making them feel uptight?

Other (perceived) stressors include moving house, divorce, starting a new job, uncertainty, social media, money issues, the climate crisis, the news, technology, lack of sleep . . .

What would be on your list?

If it's a long one, you're not alone. In my study, *91%* of people agreed that how they are feeling is determined by what is going on around them.

But consider a different reality. What if you knew that those things on your 'stress/anxiety list' have no direct power over your peace of mind and cannot rob your resilience? Imagine how much more empowered you would feel and how that could change your life.

The ultimate myth: *life is stressful*

We all have moments of feeling uptight, upset or unsettled but it turns out that most of us don't recognise the crucial role our mind plays in these feelings and responses.

Like my workplace study highlights, there's always a long list of other stuff that we believe is responsible for our stress and the role of our own mind is usually at the bottom of the list.

When you feel stressed, anxious or worried at work, what do you attribute that to?

1.	Workload	66%
2.	Pressure of deadlines	53%
3.	Not enough time	46%
4.	Other people / relationship issues	34%
5.	Poor management/leadership	34%
6.	Lack of control / responsibility	30%
7.	Uncertainty	27.5%
8.	Lack of confidence	22.1%
9.	**My own thinking / mindset**	**17.7%**
10.	Too much responsibility	6%

Let's say you're driving somewhere, and it seems like the 'idiot' who cut in front of you is the reason you're yelling and making rude hand gestures. Or you're sitting with colleagues thinking 'if only they would hurry up, I could leave this mind-numbing meeting and get on with my work'. Is your increasing frustration coming from the conversation in the room or the conversation in your head?

The idea that life is full of stressors that automatically induce anxiety is an assumption that rarely gets challenged. Instead, it gets widely promoted by organisations that we view as experts, which often makes us more likely to accept what we're told, especially when what they're saying looks and feels true to us.

In the World Health Organisation's handbook, it says:

> **'There are many causes of stress, including personal difficulties (e.g. conflict with loved ones, being alone, lack of income, worries about the future), problems at work (e.g. conflict with colleagues, an extremely demanding or insecure job) or major threats in your community (e.g. violence, disease, lack of economic opportunity).'[8]**

There's no denying that life can be challenging and full of hardship. But it's made much harder when we misunderstand the nature of our feelings and when we don't remember that resilience is a constant you can rely on.

My friend was experiencing sudden hair loss and went to see her doctor. As they explored the root cause, she said, 'I've been very anxious recently,' to which he replied 'What kind of work do you do?' On hearing her answer, he declared, 'That's definitely one of the most stressful jobs.'

Her doctor's response was coming from a compassionate place but it perpetuates the outside-in myth, which in the long term didn't serve my friend's recovery.

In 2005, writer David Foster Wallace gave a rousing speech for the graduates of Kenyon College.

He invites them to imagine a scenario where two young fish are swimming along. They happen to meet an older fish swimming in the opposite direction who greets them and asks how they're finding the water. The two fish continue swimming along until one of them asks the other, What on earth is water?[9]

We're born into the principle of *Thought* like fish are born into water.

We live and breathe *Thought* but we cannot directly see or touch it. It's like mental oxygen.

We may as well ask

'What on earth is *Thought*?'

The *Thought*–feeling connection

I was counselling Yuto, a psychologist based in Tokyo who was struggling with anxiety. He told me that throughout his years of training, thought and feeling had never been described as a unified system of experience. They had always been explained as being two separate entities.

We explored why the principle of *Thought* cannot be separated from feelings and sensations, except in your mind, because they are two sides of the same coin.

'Ah okay . . . that would be like trying to separate the scent from the flower when they go hand in hand."

I love what Yuto realised. I had never thought of it that way.

The flower produces the fragrance, just as the principle of Thought produces emotion, sensation and perception. We cannot have one without the other.

The challenge we're up against is that we think we're responding directly to a situation or a person's words or actions when, in reality, we're reacting to a flurry of activity within the mind/body system. It's the most dazzling special effects department, unmatched by even the best movie.

Jim Carrey said, 'There's a huge difference between a dog that's going to eat you in your mind and an actual dog that's going to eat you.'[10] And sometimes we confuse these two things.

Life in the boxing ring

'My mind is all over the place. I feel paralysed by the amount of work and stuff I need to deal with. I keep thinking how can I possibly do it all. I've had stressful periods but never consistently like this. I've had hot/cold sweats, shallow breathing, high blood pressure. I felt like I was drowning under the weight of it all. Being absent from my personal life, not seeing my kids or having any quality time with them . . . it feels like I am failing as a father and a husband.'

Nick was on the brink of burnout so his company agreed that he reduce his working hours and take time to rest and recover. During one of our conversations, he said, 'I'm fighting with my thoughts and feelings.' I remembered a Monty Python sketch where Colin 'Bomber' Harris is alone in a boxing ring wrestling himself.[11] The match ends with Colin knocking himself out with a right hook. I watched it with Nick and he laughed, saying 'That's me!'

We're all wrestling these imaginary opponents in the form of emotions, situations, people, the past, the future.

Nick was spending so much time worrying and overthinking. He didn't realise he was ramping up his anxiety to the point where he couldn't think clearly or function properly.

Zoe was also in her own boxing ring. She felt like she was in a 'constant battle' with 'complex challenges, demanding clients and lack of resources'. But, when she took time out to recover, she realised she'd had busy periods like this before without burning out. She said that many of her colleagues had equally busy or demanding lives and they weren't suffering like she was. As she reflected more, something occurred to her:

'How is it that some people thrive, no matter what the circumstances and other people struggle, no matter what the circumstances?'

It's such a great question. Unless we recognise the role that *Thought* is playing, that peace and well-being we're searching for ends up feeling forever out of reach and at the mercy of a million other things.

Yes but . . . if it wasn't for [my past traumas/demanding job/the climate crisis/difficult people/lack of money/health issues/screaming kids . . .], I wouldn't be thinking this way in the first place and wouldn't feel this way.

Along with friends and clients, this was something I grappled with. Like 18% of participants in my study, I was sure that attitude had a lot to do with feeling stressed or anxious, but I was also convinced that circumstances played a major part too. When I raised this with a mentor back in 2010, their response stopped me in my tracks:

'That's like saying the earth is spinning on its axis and standing still at the same time – it can't be both. The Inside>out principles are always at work just like gravity. Regardless of what you believe, and you can believe anything, our spiritual and emotional life is shaped from within, every moment that we draw breath.'

Throughout my life, I'd spent hours and days feeling worried or insecure, concerned about things that I thought had power over how I think and feel. And many of those things didn't even exist! I'd also spent a huge amount on my education and training. I was financially and emotionally invested in what I had learned. I didn't feel ready to let go of all that old knowledge. And I still had lots of 'yes buts'.

'How do I get this? I mean *really* get it?' I asked another mentor a few months later.

'It's like a butterfly. You can't make them land on you. Stop trying to get it, and just let life teach you. You'll have insights, sometimes when you least expect them. Just be open to seeing something new and try not to hold on to your ideas so tightly. The truth will find you.'

Really?! I felt short changed. At least give me a strategy, a few tips or something! Turns out they were right because, a few days later, I had a realisation. If the Inside>out principles hold true like the law of gravity, there will be no exceptions. None. And I love a challenge, so I began to look for some exceptions . . . I began trying to break the inside>out formula and find a situation where it isn't true.

Philosopher Alan Watts wisely said 'People can't be talked out of illusions. If a person believes that the earth is flat, you can't talk him out of that, he knows that it's flat. He'll go down to the window and see that it's obvious, it looks flat. So the only way to convince him that it isn't is to say, "Well let's go and find the edge".'

Let's explore some examples as you reflect on your own experience.

Consider deadlines. I have clients who say they function far better with a deadline while others say that deadlines stress them out. And what about workload? I have friends who feel anxious when they don't have enough work and others who feel anxious when they have a lot on. Each additional task feels like it might take them over the edge. So is anxiety a result of too much work or not enough?

And what about rollercoasters. An exhilarating ride or a living nightmare? Personally, I would rather hug a giant cactus, but I have friends who relish the thrill of that loop de loop.

So what accounts for these differences? Do deadlines, workload or fairground rides have the power to create feelings and sensations without the mind making it possible?

Time is an interesting one. How can a week can feel like a month and a day can feel like an hour? And you might say that it depends on whether you're having a good time or not, but no. Time flies when you're having fun and it can also seem like time slows right down. There is no rule because its always a matter of perception.

Have you ever felt overwhelmed and then a few hours later you feel calm and settled even though nothing in your outer environment has changed?

I have friends who by their own admission have comfortable lives, but they're frequently stressed, and sometimes depressed. I know others with lives that are very challenging, unpredictable and sometimes dangerous, and they live in deep levels of mental well-being.

During a chat with a doctor, they offered a great example "One of my patients, despite being in good shape, is consumed by health anxieties, so they keep visiting me for reassurance. Another patient who has quite complex health issues, is generally calm and rarely anxious."

Okay, now the serious stuff. Why does my partner's habit of leaving his underwear millimetres from the laundry bin rankle me more than a major life event? (apparently it's a Herculean task to drop it in).

During a group coaching session, Aisha tells us that mess makes her stressed and anxious. 'How does that show up day to day?' we asked.

'When I get home from a long day at work, I have to tidy everything up before I can relax or do anything else. I'm constantly telling the kids off for making a mess or shouting at them to clear up,' she says.

'And what's the impact of that?' we asked. 'I'm distracted, on edge and not present with my family. I'm probably not much fun to be around, if I'm honest.'

It also dawned on her that it wasn't just affecting her home life. She explained that when there's a lot of paperwork on her desk, her 'mess' alarm gets triggered and she feels overwhelmed, often spiralling into anxiety.

'What is mess?' we ask the group. Sam says a messy home reminds her that 'life is happening'. Krista says 'mess means we're relaxed!'. Aisha thinks they must be joking. She can't believe that something she gets so uptight about can be comforting to someone else. But when you think about it, mess like any pet peeve, is in the mind of the perceiver. That's why one person's mess is another's chilled vibe.

We are constantly creating and assigning meaning to everything. Nothing has any independent meaning without the principle of *Thought* being involved.

A few weeks later the group is back together. I ask Aisha how things have been. With a big smile she says 'Would you believe it? I went away with the family and when we got home, I left my bags untouched for an entire week!' Everyone is laughing now, including Aisha.

She carries on, 'I know it sounds like "so what", but for me it was a big deal! Usually, I'd be knee deep in laundry within an hour of being home even if it's 1 am. This time, my family were shocked at how relaxed I was. They kept asking if I was OK! I just had more important things to do like catch up with people and get some sleep. My kids say I'm much nicer to be around and I enjoy being at home now.'

Take a moment . . .

What's your version of 'mess'?

What are those things that seem to stress you out or create anxiety?

Are there any repetitive concerns or worries that seem to drain your energy or deplete your resilience?

Are there situations or circumstances that you've automatically labelled as stressful?

Your mind creates connections between how you think, feel and behave.

Example: *mess = stress = low mood*

Useful distinction:
causation vs correlation

You're aware of two or more things happening at the same time and you make a mental leap or assumption that one is causing the other.

For example, you're sitting on a rollercoaster strapped into your seat, waiting for the ride to begin. Your palms start to sweat, your heart begins to race. You think the rollercoaster ride is doing that to you. But just because you are sitting on a rollercoaster *and* your heart is racing does not mean that one is causing the other.

Or you're about to make a speech. Your mouth is getting dry and your hands are clammy. You start feeling anxious. You get more and more self-conscious. You think it's because of the event and the people. But, like the rollercoaster, just because you're giving a talk *and* there are feelings of anxiety, doesn't mean that one is causing the other. It also doesn't mean there is anything wrong with having those feelings.

Taking this all into account, here's how the experience of anxiety, stress and all feelings get created;

Universal Principles of Mind + Thought + Consciousness

+ how we think stress/anxiety works

= current state of consciousness (emotions, sensations, chemistry, perceptions, mood, attitude, reality)

which in turn generates our responses, actions, behaviour.

Anxiety is an intense feeling of worry that can lead to panic attacks. And what I've learned is that panic attacks aren't the problem. It's the fear of having one, because the symptoms, such as a racing heart or shortness of breath, often freak people out. And so it becomes a self-reinforcing cycle.

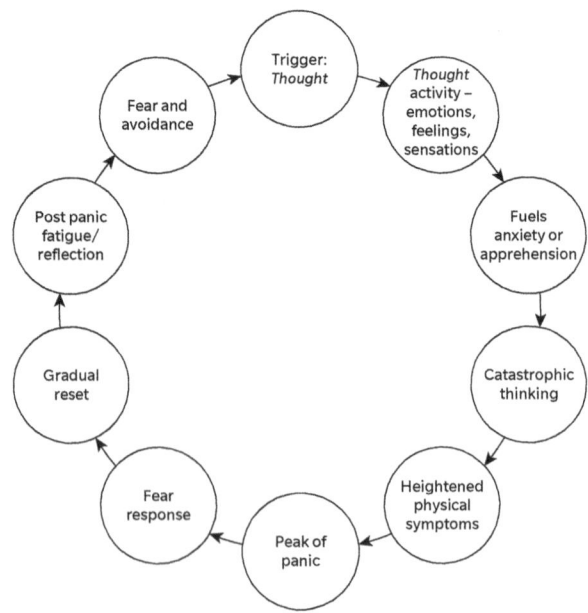

Cliff thought that networking and meeting new people were the reason for his anxiety. To cope with his feelings he would avoid those situations. That's an example of 1st order change because it tweaks behaviour to alleviate symptoms in the short term, but doesn't address the root cause.

My friend Jules was anxious about driving on motorways, so she took the scenic route, adding 45 minutes to her journey each day. And she was already struggling to balance work and home life. This detour meant less time with her kids which added worry and guilt to an already heavy heart.

If we don't include the power of *Thought* in our experience of stress or anxiety (or any feeling state), we won't have an accurate view of what's happening. We end up deluding ourselves and wondering why we feel so shitty or why the situation seems worse. But when you remember what's happening behind the scenes, the spiralling stops and you regain your bearings.

Yes but . . . if everyone agrees that something is overwhelming, how can everyone be wrong? Some people lose their job or their home so, of course, they will feel anxious about it.

This isn't saying that feelings are wrong or unjustified. This isn't about what you should or shouldn't think and feel. It's about the nature of *Thought* and how feelings and emotions come into existence and what we make them mean.

The family of Ruth Perry, said that teaching had been Ruth's mission and passion for 32 years until tragically, she took her own life on 8th January 2023, leaving behind a grieving family.

Ruth's sister acknowledged that there may have been other contributing factors but also said that their family had no doubt that her death was the direct result of the pressure placed on her by Ofsted,[12] the schools' watchdog, through their inspection process and imminent downgrading of Ruth Perry's school.

A petition[13] calling for an inquiry into this particular case said the following;

"Ofsted inspections have evolved into such a monster that the mere thought of them causes fear, stress and anxiety to schools, school leadership and staff alike. Actual inspections can leave staff in tears.

"Many leaders leave the profession following an inspection because the stress caused by the inspection is simply too great and sadly some take their own life, like in the very sad case of Ruth Perry."

Notice the language. An inspection is a 'monster'. The 'mere thought' causes fear and anxiety. The Inside>out principle (and the outside>in illusion) is right here in plain sight.

Here's what a colleague of mine who worked in education for many years said:

'The school was evaluated and given a score. The evaluation may well have been disproportionate, poorly evidenced or badly handled. And this should be challenged and addressed. But Ofsted's inspections and evaluations do not have the power to decide how we perceive and respond to them. Many of us who work in schools and social care have seen staff become frantic or highly anxious when Ofsted is coming in. But we've also seen that when people feel emotionally secure and supported, it's easier for them to keep their bearings and work through these situations.'

We're going to experience whatever feelings are moving through us in any moment. Like lenses, these feelings are colouring and shaping how the situation appears to you. That's why you can have such wildly different perspectives in the same circumstances and also from other people in the same situation. This tragic loss of life is an extreme consequence of mental hijack created by the outside<in illusion.

But if we don't remember this and other people express a similar view or feeling, it reinforces our thinking. For example, you're sitting in the pub with friends and everyone agrees that losing a job is depressing or job interviews are highly stressful. It's easy to get drawn into a false reality. But just because there's agreement, doesn't make it true.

'We first raise the dust, then complain we cannot see'
George Berkeley, Irish philosopher
(1685–1753)

Let's say you're moving home and you start worrying; 'Aaaaghr, there's so much to do, how will I cope with it all!' or it falls through and you're distraught. You say to yourself 'Why is this happening to me. It's so unfair!'. The distress spirals and in that moment it really seems like your feelings and reactions are coming from the situation itself. You tell a friend how depressed you feel and they say, 'remember that moving home is one of the most stressful things, so of course you're going to feel this way.'

We mean well when we say these things to each other, but what we're doing is breathing life into our feelings of helplessness. There is no situation that can independently control how you feel, respond or behave. But conditioning and group think is compelling and sometimes damaging.

In the words of philosopher Ludwig Wittgenstein:

'Nothing is so difficult as not deceiving oneself.'[14]

An example of this deception is 'Blue Monday'. It's alleged that a travel company decided to spread an idea that the third Monday in January is the most depressing day of the year. Media outlets promoted it. It caught on and a passing thought went viral and became a fact. Each year, I'm sure it will go away and then I get an email saying something like 'how to make your Blue Monday brighter' with a bunch of discount codes for more stuff that I don't need.

But how does a date in the diary make us feel something without our mind being the active agent?

We come into the world as a thinker and feeler.

Your mind projects those moment-to-moment feelings and perceptions onto a situation, a person, a past or future event.

A temporary thought or feeling gets objectified and turned into a thing. And now those 'things' that no longer look like *Thought* get labelled as stressful, anxiety provoking or overwhelming. And they become the reason and target for our (apparent) inability to reset.

Social media is a powerful example of this. Many young people are harming themselves because they feel victimised by this virtual world that they're spending a significant portion of their lives living in.

There's no question that there is a ton of abuse happening online. People hiding behind fake names, projecting their self-loathing and insecurity onto others. And that's why it's crucial to understand that likes, follows and ignorant or unkind comments have no ultimate power over our mental life. That power can only exist as a perception taking form in our minds and bodies.

It's undeniable that every day, in every part of the world, people are facing difficulty or danger including abuse, oppression, earthquakes, homelessness, starvation and war. These situations are real. Emotions and feelings are real. What's not real is the idea that you can be made to think, feel or act in a particular way without a mind to make those feelings, perceptions or actions possible in the first place.

But we can easily feel mentally or physically hijacked by the intensity of emotions and physical sensations, to the degree that we lose perspective or can't function. That's why it's so important and helpful to understand what's happening behind the scenes.

Awareness and understanding is the antidote to chronic stress and anxiety. Only then can we find our bearings, make good decisions, act with compassion, and reduce unnecessary or prolonged suffering.

Burnout among social workers is reportedly very high compared to other sectors. Their day-to-day work can be very challenging and complex. They support people who are dealing with homelessness, addiction, abuse and mental health issues. They're making decisions that change people's lives, which often includes removing children from families as a last resort. Here's what Jo, a child protection worker said:

'When I visit families, I have some difficult and sometimes aggressive behaviour that I have to face. In the past, I would often feel sick with anxiety before I had even parked my car. By the time I got to their front door I was in such a state that I would rush through the meeting so I could get out as quickly as possible. I knew this wasn't helpful for me or for them . . .

'. . . then I learned that my feelings of anxiety were coming from within my own thought system. It wasn't about the angry dad. It wasn't them at all. I had a lot of repetitive and judgemental thinking about the parents and their situation. I constantly second guessed my ability to do the job and that's why I felt so stressed and overwhelmed . . .

'. . . the more I noticed what was really going on, the more settled I became. Now when I visit a family, I feel much calmer. I know I'm there to help and understand.

'Their anger and frustration is coming from their own insecurities and worries. I get that now, so I have more empathy. I don't take people's anger or upset personally and this means I can think more clearly and listen properly. These relationships are improving and I'm better at my job now.'

It's not personal

As Nick began to recognise how much time he'd been spending in the boxing ring and how those anxious feelings were thought based and not situation based, he said *'I've created so much stress for myself'*.

We talked about why it's important to remember that it's not personal. What I mean is that we don't wake up and think 'today I am going to make myself feel like sh*t'. As we explored in the previous chapter, we don't choose feelings of anxiety or overwhelm. We don't choose to have panic attacks. It's just that we don't always notice that we've been ruminating, worrying or fighting with our thinking – sometimes for hours or days on end.

When we don't realise this, we risk becoming our own biggest stressor! It's like we've taken the stick out of someone else's hand and now we are beating ourselves with it instead. That's why it's helpful to become more conscious of what's happening on the inside.

Learning to read the signs

I was driving somewhere and got to a junction to find it had been blocked off due to road works. Where were the signs to tell me there was a diversion?! Why can't people just do their job properly?! As I turned the car round and headed back, I noticed two *big* signs saying 'road ahead closed'. I was so busy in my head that I missed the warning and ended up down a dead end. Ever done that? ☺

If you think about the role of a car dashboard, it's there to give us important feedback about what's going on inside the engine. It tells you when to slow down, refuel, recharge, or check your tyres. To use any feedback system wisely, we need to understand what it's telling us.

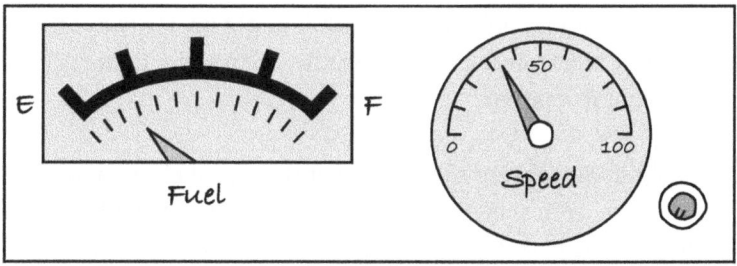

Like the dashboard your mind and body sends signs and signals to let you know if you need to rest or reset. If you're overthinking, you'll know because you might feel mentally exhausted or overwhelmed. If you're pushing yourself too hard and not resting enough, feelings of fatigue or frustration could be telling you to slow down and take care of yourself.

Sometimes, I realise I've been stewing on something for a while. I might notice some tension or anxiety. It's easy to forget that we're in an experience of *Thought* creating feeling. That's why it's so helpful to listen to the feedback your mind/body system is giving you.

If I notice that I'm getting short tempered, or losing my compassion or sense of humour, these are helpful signs that I probably need to stop and recalibrate. Often, just noticing is enough.

What are some signs that let you know you might be heading down an outside-in rabbit hole?

Blaming workload, money issues or the climate crisis for your current state of mind is like blaming the car in front for your empty fuel tank. This misplaced reasoning hijacks our common sense. We give our power away while we search for solace and solutions in all the wrong places.

This doesn't mean these situations aren't happening. Or that we should just accept how things are. Many people have crazy out of whack workloads. Some people are struggling to pay their bills. There is a climate and ecological emergency. But our capacity to handle any situation, however difficult it might be, is always there. We just forget that sometimes. Especially when we're in the grip of extreme mental weather.

As a teenager, Steve went through several years of emotional and physical abuse from someone close to him. When we met he said "I will never let the past determine my future. Yes, it happened, but it has no power to control or define me, except the power I give it'.

Both Nick and Zoe had felt so mentally overwhelmed that they temporarily lost their capacity to think straight. But by understanding the true nature of stress, their relationship with work changed. Nick began to feel more at ease. Instead of incessantly worrying or over-analysing, he's able to think through things, without old reactions clouding his judgement. And, when those old thought habits kick in, he catches on to them faster. He began pushing back and setting clearer work/home boundaries for himself. Instead of being drawn into the drama like he would have been, he guides his colleagues out of choppy mental waters, back to shore.

Zoe began to feel mentally settled. The noise began to quieten and her energy returned. She said that even in those darker moments, she knew she wasn't broken.

Resilience shows itself in many ways and in Zoe's case that included a forced stop and a time of deep reflection and insight. It wasn't too long before she returned to her role, but with a new perspective and a deeper appreciation for how we are designed to thrive.

Feelings aren't facts. Feelings are feedback about the activity of our Thought system.

> **'Until Thought is understood – better yet, more than understood, perceived – it will actually control us; but it will create the impression that it is our servant, that it is just doing what we want it to do. That's the difficulty. Thought is participating and then saying it's not participating. But it is taking part in everything.'**
>
> **Professor David Bohm**[15]

How we think about stress or anxiety, has the strongest impact on how we experience it. This includes how your body is affected. But it's not just stress. The degree to which any feeling or perception affects you is a direct result of how you think *Thought* and reality works. When we think that something beyond our mind can control how we feel and behave, that 'thing' automatically becomes the target of our attention.

In my own study,[16] we found some interesting and significant correlations that evidenced this.

Those who agreed that stress is circumstantial tend to feel more stressed, anxious and worried. Those who agreed that stress originates from within the mind, feel less stressed, anxious and worried.

(95% significance level)

My stepdad had cancer several years ago. His spleen was removed, along with a sizeable tumour. Since then, he's had various health challenges including IBS. One day, he said, 'Do you think my anxiety is making my symptoms worse?'

Until this point, he was sure his anxiety was *because* of his health issues. For the first time, he was considering that it could also be the other way around. He asked me what he should do. I suggested he get curious and notice when he's actively worrying about his ailments. This included how much time he spent thinking about how horrible he felt. There were signs he could easily recognise. And because I wanted him to just notice without judging, I asked him to imagine he was a scientist doing some research on the mind.

'The range of what we think and do is limited by what we fail to notice. And because we fail to notice that we fail to notice there is little we can do to change until we notice how failing to notice shapes our thoughts and deeds.'

Daniel Goleman[17]

The wisdom of the system

Symptoms of stress and anxiety are messengers. They're a gift. Just as pain signals give you vital feedback, emotional suffering is doing the same. This is the wisdom of the system.

Your feelings - mental and physical - are alerting you to how you are using the inside>out principles. And like our physical form, the mind has its own immune system . . . a self-righting capacity that returns to its original state of stillness and sanity. And there is nothing that you have to do for this to happen. It's part of nature's design.

In essence

- ♥ We're always living in the feelings and sensations brought to life through Consciousness in each moment
- ♥ Resilience is not the absence of anxious or stressful feelings. It's the capacity to be with all feelings, knowing you can function well despite your moment to moment states of mind.
- ♥ Feelings of stress or anxiety are messengers. They don't need to be feared. Feelings are feedback about the activity of your Thought system.

Bonus chapter materials here: http://www.chantalburns.com/ bulletproof-chapter-5-freedom-from-stress-anxiety-and-burnout

The wisdom of the system

chapter 6

The myth of me

'Who we are is a story, a narrative
we construct,
and like any other story, it can change
and evolve over time.'

Salman Rushdie

Who are you?

It might seem like a strange question but think about it for a moment.

Would you start with your name? Would you describe your heritage or maybe your likes and dislikes? Would you focus on job role, gender, personality, religious beliefs or something else?

How you relate to this idea of 'me' influences every aspect of your life. And self-image is *the* greatest source of mental interference because most of what you think about, in some way, relates to defending, protecting or validating this sense of self.

But what if this 'me' that seems so fixed, is in fact fluid? What if the 'me' you see in the mirror, that chats away to you all day, is more than personality, genes or past personal history?

We come into the world as 'wisps of undifferentiated nothingness' as writer Kurt Vonnegut puts it.[1] For several months, there is no awareness of a 'me' but from the moment we are named, a sense of identity and a (perceived) separate self is created. Or perhaps even earlier, as people often start charting our lives before we're born.

It's in those earliest years when we're most vulnerable and reliant on others to help and guide us. We trust (often unconditionally) those who have most influence over our growing sense of self. Their ideas, beliefs, anxieties and dreams become part of our developing *Thought* system. They become part of your story of 'me'.

Growing up, what did you learn or decide about yourself and the world?

What have you learned to believe about this self that you've come to know?

For example, did you learn that you can be anything and do anything? Were you given the idea that you were more deserving than others, even put on a pedestal to the point of entitlement? Were you encouraged and comforted or were you criticised and told you were a worthless waste of space? Did you grow up around people who were loving, fearless and trusting, who encouraged the same in you? Or were your formative years framed by fear, aggression or self-doubt?

Innocent lies we tell ourselves

When I was a teenager, I had lots of insecurities and limiting beliefs . . . about my appearance, my capability, how others perceived me. Many continued into adult life. Some of these ideas took root at school, sitting on the cold tarmac waiting for the netball captain to pick her team . . . always the last to be chosen. Maybe it was because I was smaller than the other girls. Perhaps I just looked defeated. Who knows. But I was also the girl who had stabilisers on her bike until she was 12 and came off it more than I stayed on. At some point, the idea 'I'm not sporty' took hold and became part of my identity. Anything even remotely athletic or outdoorsy got zero interest from me.

When I turned 40, I signed up for a 10k run. I couldn't even run for a bus without hyperventilating, so this was major for me. I completed my 10k in just over an hour without collapsing. But what did collapse were some old stories and, with them, all the insecure thinking and behaviour attached to them.

We construct, collect and connect ideas about ourselves and the world. Some of these ideas celebrate your potential. They liberate and inspire you. Others will be limiting or even debilitating.

> **'Reality is a creation of the mind. It cannot exist independently of the mind that perceives it.'**
>
> **Einstein**

Being independent has been a key part of my self-image. An attitude handed down from my Mum, who by necessity, learned to be self-sufficient from a young age. By eleven, I was earning pocket money by washing hair on the weekends at a local salon and at 14, I convinced a major department store that I was old enough to be hired. I was determined to get a job and not have to rely on anyone else for money.

All of this reinforced my growing sense of self-reliance. But there are downsides. I'm still not great at asking for help, even when I need it. In my head, needing help meant 'I'm not good enough' or not capable, so I had to constantly prove otherwise.

While writing this book, it dawned on me that I'd equated being resilient with going it alone. Ironic, given how my life is all about supporting others. Being able and willing to ask for help is not just a strength; it's essential. Fostering resilient communities is more crucial than ever.

If you had asked me a few years ago if I was an activist, I would have said no. I had a very fixed idea of what an activist was. And then, one day, I found myself campaigning and protesting to keep our local railway crossing open – a lifeline for locals. Within a week, we had a campaign team and a Facebook group with over 500 residents. We petitioned the council, did a ton of research and began speaking on the radio. Eighteen months later, we won our campaign. That experience completely changed how I think about activism and all the other labels and stories we sign up to about who we are and what we are capable of.

Activism is just another label or category made of *Thought* and expressed through language and behaviour. If we saw activism simply as being active in ways that matter most to you, then a passionate parent could describe themselves as an activist when they campaign for better school facilities.

*What are some of the stories, ideas and beliefs you've most closely identified with, which became part of your **I am** or **I'm not** story?*

What changes would you love to make? What possibilities would you love to create in the world but perhaps you've been stopping yourself because you thought 'that's not who I am' or 'I can't because I'm not ___ or I am ___'?

What if these reasons are not who you are but simply how you are thinking about who you are, in each moment?

'In order to find yourself, who you really are, you need to let go of everything you think you know about yourself.'

Werner Ehrhard[2]

One of the most widely accepted ideas that contributes to the story of 'me' is the one about character or personality.

The myth of personality

Dr Benjamin Hardy, author of *Personality isn't Permanent*, says, 'There are two types of people in the world: those who believe there are two types of people in the world, and those who don't.'[3]

This myth is made up of three false assumptions:

- *Personality is predetermined (via genes/DNA).*
- *There are some core 'types' or categories that we all fit into.*
- *Your character or personality is 'who you are'.*

Typology, including personality profiling, is a multi-million dollar industry, used for counselling, recruitment, dating, team and personal development. It's popular because we want to understand ourselves better. And, let's be honest, most people love talking about themselves ☺

I've facilitated numerous sessions using tools like this. With increasing awareness, we can have more insightful, honest and open conversations together. We get to know each other at a deeper level. But this is only useful if it's grounded in reality.

I was walking through the reception of an organisation a few years ago and I happened to notice a staff directory on the screen and, next to their names were letters, representing their 'personality type'. My heart sank a little. This wasn't how they were intended to be used.

Here are some of the unintended consequences of personality profiling:

- If you think the profile is who you are, or a character trait is fixed rather than a fluid form of *Thought*, you might also assume that change isn't possible. As a result, you might not even attempt to make changes.

- At the very least, you might be less open to perspectives that challenge your self-image, further limiting potential.

- You might miss opportunities because you believe you don't have the 'right personality' for whatever it is.

- When we label or categorise others and see them only as that label, we're distorting our own perception of *their* potential. We might even write people off because we think we know who they are or what they are capable of.

How often do you judge or justify yours or someone else's potential or behaviour based on a personality type? We say things like 'I'm not a people person. I'm an introvert. That's why I acted that way.' But one has nothing to do with the other. And, more importantly, it's all a fabrication.

It's true that you might feel more suited or attracted to some situations, hobbies, jobs or people, but your mind creates far more constraints than actually exist.

In 1921, Carl Jung came up with the original 'types' that formed part of one of the most popular profiling tests, Myers Briggs (MBTI). 'There is no such thing as a pure extravert or a pure introvert,' Jung stated. He also said that, 'Every individual is an exception to the rule,' meaning there is no rule.

Throughout history, we've learned how typecasting can lead to unhelpful bias, prejudice and stereotypes that major on difference instead of seeing our shared humanity. Interestingly, if you search for words that mean the *opposite* of 'typecasting', it offers up 'truth'.

Yes but . . . I do respond in a very similar way in certain situations. For example, I'm always competitive. It's part of my personality.

Conditioning is a powerful process. The brain learns fast, generating patterns, preferences or thinking habits. And sometimes those patterns of thinking get mistaken for who we are, rather than how we think about who we are.

Suzy wanted to build deeper connections with people, including colleagues. When I asked 'what's stopping you?', she said 'because I'm shy'.

She felt awkward and insecure in social situations, sometimes to the point of paranoia. She avoided events where she would have to engage with people she didn't know. And with people she knew fairly well, she held back from sharing too much of herself.

For as long as she could remember, Suzy was sure that her shyness was a fact . . . a fixed part of her genetic make-up. But as we explored her story, she realised something that changed her life.

Shyness is not a permanent condition. It's a *Thought* habit.

If we frequently think about ourselves or the world in a particular way, it becomes a pattern of thinking and part of our self-image. And this also leads to repetitive behaviour that reinforces those ideas. But when you put *Thought* back into the experience equation, it brings you back to what is true.

Using Suzy's example below, put any word inside the brackets below so it's relevant to your own experience.

Outside<in idea	Inside>out fact
I am [shy]	I'm a thinker that can think anything
It's just the way I am	thoughts/feelings occur,
that's why I feel and behave like this	which the mind interprets and labels as [shy]
	and we think, feel and act in accordance with that idea / belief / story.

It's true that we can think of ourselves as having a type, a style or preferred way of being, but these types and preferences are perception.

Here's what a friend's daughter shared recently:

'A few years ago, my grandparents moved into a care home. My grandpa has always been sociable and outgoing, so he was keen to get involved with all the activities on offer. My grandma, on the other hand, not so much! A more reserved soul, she's always struggled in social situations.

'Before their move, she was diagnosed with dementia, and as time passed, it really took hold, making her memory fleeting . . . events fading away after a few days.

'Dementia can make family life incredibly hard, and part of me feels uneasy about saying this . . . but I can't deny the truth that my grandma has become happier. Infinitely so. She has a deep contentment she never possessed before. It's as if a new version of herself has been unlocked . . . a version that was always there but constrained by all those old ideas about herself. And now it's like she's completely free. Instead of turning down an activity because 'that's not my thing', she's up for everything! She embraces it all with a childlike enthusiasm. You should see her. Art class, Pilates, choir, you name it, she's in. She even loves singing in the choir. She would never have considered it before, always insisting she was 'tone deaf'. But I heard her sing recently and she's no Adele but, you know what, she sounds OK! Her memory might be fading but her joy is increasing.

'My grandma's journey is teaching me that who we are is an ever-changing idea and what we thought was a terrible fate is bringing unexpected gifts.'

MBTI is still popular with organisations but most psychologists no longer use it as it has no reliable scientific basis. As Dr Benjamin Hardy described, 'It feels scientific, but really it's just superstition dressed up as science.'

I used to love using tools like this, and they were well received by clients. But once you know something is fundamentally untrue, however interesting and popular it might be, it's hard to get behind it.

The way you complete any questionnaire depends on what you perceive as relevant, important or true *in that moment*, including any conditioning and bias we've acquired over time.

> **'Thought is creating divisions out of itself and then saying that they are there naturally.'**
>
> **David Bohm**

All categories are a generalisation based on observing differences in attitude and behaviour across multiple contexts. But the idea that there are pre-existing categories that we neatly fit into is false. And the results demonstrate this. When people retake the test again after five weeks, there's up to a 50% chance it will give you a different profile.[4] This becomes problematic if the test is sold as giving you a reliably consistent profile, i.e. one that doesn't change. But when you consider this from the inside>out, change is inevitable because what we think and feel is always changing. The only constant is the fact of the principle of *Thought* itself.

Adam Grant, professor of Psychology at Wharton said, 'The characteristics measured by the test have almost no predictive power on how happy you'll be in a situation, how you'll perform at your job, or how happy you'll be in your marriage.'

We use these tests to alleviate uncertainty and to predict what we'll think, feel or do in some future moment. But this isn't possible because the most important part – what we will think and feel in the moment – is always missing from any model.

The essence of who we are cannot be summed up by four letters or any other label, even dickhead, a personal favourite.

Which brings us to an important question.

Do genes determine character?

You might be wondering where genetics fit into all of this. Are we genetically programmed to think or behave in a particular way? Is there any aspect of your character that's inherited or pre-determined?

The science seems clear. Genes do not cause character, but they can influence it, which is a crucial difference.

Pre-disposition is not the same as a fixed and unchangeable personality.

Well that's a relief, otherwise I really am screwed :)

We inherit genes but we don't inherit how they get expressed.

Our genes may or may not get activated during our lifetime. This means that genetically identical twins can have distinctly different personalities or character traits, despite living in the same home and having the same upbringing.

The idea that DNA is in the driving seat of who and how we are, has been disproved many times. Epigenetics, the frontier of genetic science, sheds fascinating light on how our use of the principle of *Thought* influences genetic expression.

As we explored in an earlier chapter, one of the most telling examples of how the mind can influence our biology is with the placebo effect.

'The brain is like a chemist. The brain secretes the chemistry into the blood that changes the fate of the cells. But the brain doesn't do this automatically. It does it in connection with our mind, our beliefs, and our perceptions.'

Bruce Lipton, cellular biologist and author[5]

No IQ gene has been found. There is no introvert gene. There's no shyness gene. There's no 'task focused' gene. There's no Jewish, Muslim, Christian or any other religious gene. There's no dick-head gene (sorry but it's true) and there is no resilience gene.

Genes don't determine personality or character. But the stories we tell ourselves about genetics, ability and personality will inevitably influence how we relate to this sense of 'self' and 'other'. And it's always shaping how we think about our capacity to thrive and change.

Fact. You don't come into the world as practical, loyal or driven. But when someone shows up as ambitious, we say that's who they are . . . that's their personality. We then try to predict their feelings or behaviour based on that label. We also justify or explain our own or other people's behaviour by those labels. For example, 'I'm always blunt. It's just the way I am. I can't change.' Or 'I'm an introvert so that's why I'm not comfortable in those situations.'

The labels we create and assign seem to give us comfort. Like a diagnosis, we might get a perceived sense of certainty about who we are or why we behave the way we do. You might feel constrained or limited by that label or description or you might feel liberated.

'Diagnostic questionnaires don't "reveal" pathology. They order people into disorder categories. The more people captured by these categories, the more real the "disorders" appear to be.'

James Davies PhD.

Here are some common characterisations, viewed through an inside>out lens.

You can apply the same logic to any typology:

People pleaser

This isn't a personality type. It's a misattribution of feeling.

We believe our feelings of self-esteem and self-worth come from what others think of us, so we bend over backwards to appease, appeal or get approval. But how someone else perceives us has no bearing on our sense of self or emotional well-being, unless we think it does.

We also try to comfort or please people to make them happier. In reality, we have no ultimate control over this.

Fixer/helper

Many of us get a sense of satisfaction from being that person who saves the day. People who consider themselves fixers are connecting their feelings and perceptions with the act of helping or solving problems.

Helping others is a compassionate act and something we need in our communities. But when we think our behaviour can validate or invalidate who we are, or increase feelings of security and happiness, we will do more (or less) of that behaviour, even if it's detrimental to ourselves or others. We'll often do whatever it takes to defend, protect and maintain a self-concept or image that seems real.

Introvert, extravert, amiable, idealist, Buddhist, completer-finisher . . .

It's common for people to assign labels to themselves. Like Suzy who identified with being shy, she also saw herself as an introvert. In reality, we can think and behave in infinite ways. But mental habits or preferences get created over time, which drives behaviour and becomes part of the 'who I am' story.

You might be thinking that 'Buddhist' doesn't belong there because it's a religion. But you're not a laptop, pre-loaded with software. You don't come into the world with a set of beliefs already installed.

Religion is an example of a belief system that may well be inherited but is not genetic or predetermined. Religion is a construct that becomes (quite literally) the gospel. It's a powerful story that gets passed down via *Thought*, through generations. Then we use these crafted stories and other beliefs to generate and justify the rules and values we choose to live by.

Belief systems such as religion give people a sense of meaning and purpose. Something to hold onto. And, for many, this feels comforting or healing. But we also use religious stereotypes to justify prejudice and hate. And at the extreme end of the spectrum, these beliefs are used to justify war, cruelty and oppression. As British writer and journalist Gary Younge said; 'race is not real, but racism is'.[6]

The word personality comes from the Latin *persona*, a mask worn by an actor to project or express something. But there's a difference between who you are *at* your *core* and *who you think you are*, i.e. the various mental masks you wear.

Your view of 'self' is just that. It's pure perception. It's a projection of your personal use of the *im*personal power of *Thought* and *Consciousness*.

Instead of 'I am' it may be more accurate, and therefore helpful, to say, 'I *think* I am . . . '

Kate's self-image was built on the idea of being the 'expert'. And this meant having all the answers, always being prepared and getting things right. She told me she was a serial overthinker and described this as the 'beast I need to domesticate'.

This meant:

- She felt compelled to prove herself. She would take over, dominate or take on more than was required or necessary. This happened at work and at home. She believed that everything was her responsibility even if it wasn't. Instead of igniting people's potential – whether it was her team or her kids – she was choking their capacity to learn and develop. She tried to solve everyone's issues, even if they didn't ask.

- She would try and plan for every conceivable scenario, to cover all the bases to make sure she was ready and had the answers. This kept her mind very busy and overburdened. She believed that not having the answers and not being sure was a sign of weakness. "To be expert, you must have certainty" she told me.

For Kate, this was all about being of value. She thought depth of knowledge was evidence of her worth. She came to realise that no amount of 'expertise' or knowledge was going to satisfy her because self-worth comes from within.

'I noticed how exhausted I was . . . watching myself . . . watching this person trying so hard to be the expert, trying to get everything right and prove myself. No wonder I felt so overwhelmed,' she told me during a session.

Kate later realised that it's OK not to know. 'After all, how can we know everything?' she told me.

Like many of us, Kate believed that her thinking was an accurate description of who she is. For example, "I'm a perfectionist" seemed like a fact of life. When she saw that it was just an idea she'd signed up to, she unsubscribed and stopped taking herself so seriously. And this brought more lightness and joy into her life.

We all have ideas about ourselves, some of which get crafted over time, often out of conscious awareness. Those ideas influence the actions we do or don't take and determine what we think is possible (or not).

Identity at its essence is any label or description (crafted by *Thought*) that you relate to as being 'who I am'. Here are some examples from clients:

lazy, weird, fussy, fixer, helper, god-fearing, activist, worrier, leader, religious, empath, extravert, doer, mum, fragile, spiritual, adventurous, skeptic, perfectionist.

Take a moment . . .

What are some ways of thinking about your 'self' that have shaped how you live your life?

What labels have you subscribed to?

What judgements have you made about yourself? or accepted by others as being who you are?

How has this way of thinking informed and shaped the way you've lived your life so far?

In what ways have these labels, ideas or stories liberated you?

And in what ways have they constrained how you live your life? (perhaps in your relationships, or the decisions you have made until now).

Have you ever considered that your sense of 'self' isn't confined to, or determined by the ever-changing thoughts and emotions passing through you?

In the book *The Man Who Mistook His Wife for a Hat* by Oliver Sacks[7] (a brilliant book if you haven't read it), he shares a story about someone who can't remember or recognise anyone, including himself. So, he (unconsciously) creates multiple stories about who he is and what he's done throughout his life, believing it all to be real.

It struck me that we're all doing this. We are continually inventing who we are and what the world is and then we express those invented realities through our thoughts, feelings, sensations, language and actions. Except that like this man, we've forgotten that we are constantly creating and playing a character in this cosmic game called Life.

Where is this self that we get so attached to? Where is this self that we protect and nurture or obsess over? A separate 'me' cannot be found in the brain. Self only exists as a moment-to-moment experience of *Thought* brought to life in *Consciousness*.

> **Consciousness comes prior to physics, comes prior to science – the only way we can experience the world is through Consciousness.**

Christof Koch, neuroscientist[8]

At the most elemental level, we are the same. We are one singular *true identity* with billions of different stories.

Self is meaning we have made, using the mind, which leads to the creation of beliefs and conclusions about who you are.

Self is the ultimate personalised product of the energy and power of *Thought*.

'. . . for all those years of my life, i really had been a figment of my own imagination!'[9]

**Jill Bolte Taylor, My Stroke of Insight:
A Brain Scientist's Personal Journey**

You are not your conditioning.
You are not your past.
You are not your body.
You are not a set of traits.
You are not your failures or successes.
You are not your thoughts or your emotions.

Who you are at your essence is beyond any habitual or biological responses. Your true identity is deeper than any label, category or self-concept you might have inherited or signed up to.

It's in the boundless realm of *Mind* that every label, category, or type finds its origins.

While I was writing this book, I realised that even the notion of being a 'resilient person' is untrue, because resilience is not about personality. It's not a personal achievement. It's a spiritual gift within everyone.

There's a beautiful book called *Zoom* where as you turn each page, more and more of the picture is revealed.[10] What if we could do the same and keep zooming out until 'me' is just a tiny part of a much bigger picture. It makes you wonder, how far out can the zoom go? What if it's infinite? What if there are no boundaries to what we can realise or discover? After all, who decides the boundaries? *Thought* does!

George Bernard Shaw said, 'Life isn't about finding yourself. Life is about creating yourself.' Who you are and how you are is not pre-defined or pre-determined. Your true essence cannot be captured in words, pictures or even in feelings. You're not a book that's been written or a painting that's complete. You're a work in progress, a life story being created breath by breath, thought by thought, moment by moment. To know this, is true freedom.

In essence

- -

- ♥ Resilience exists before personality.
- ♥ Personality is not a pre-existing, permanent condition, it's a story.
- ♥ The ideas and concepts we have about ourselves are never fixed and cannot define or limit us.
- ♥ Personality and self-image is not a product of genes, it's a product of the Inside>out principles.
- ♥ Self is the personalisation of the impersonal power of *Thought*. There cannot be a 'me' without *Mind*.
- ♥ You are not your thinking . . . you are unfolding potential in every moment.

Bonus chapter materials here: http://www.chantalburns.com/bulletproof-chapter-6-the-myth-of-personality/

chapter 7

Courageous conversations

'Whenever two people meet, there are really six people present.
There is each person as they see themselves,
each person as the other sees them,
and each person as they really are.'

William James
[Adapted]

Before you read this chapter, complete this free quiz:
http://www.chantalburns.com/bulletproof-
courageous-conversations-quiz

Dan gets anxious about any kind of confrontation at school and swallows his feelings which build up like a pressure cooker, erupting in frustration at home. His parents want to help but don't know how.

Lucy hears feedback or criticism as a personal attack. If you challenge her thinking, she puts on her armour and prepares for battle. Her walls go up and she finds a way to shut the conversation down.

Rachel is the local mood manager, constantly concerned about whether her kids, friends or colleagues are OK. 'It's exhausting holding all this concern for everyone. I can't help it. It's just who I am,' she says.

Do you want to be less preoccupied by what others think of you? Do you worry too much about hurting people's feelings? Do you wish you could speak your mind more freely or like me, hold back sometimes?

Do you want to feel less affected by other people's moods or behaviour without becoming detached? Or maybe you want to be less judgemental and have more empathy.

I've dodged or delayed plenty of important conversations. Whether it was giving or getting feedback, asking for help or broaching sensitive issues. I've stayed in relationships well past their prime and put up with poor treatment when I should have spoken sooner.

'The single biggest problem in communication is the illusion that it has taken place.'

George Bernard Shaw

We hide behind devices and screens, living our lives through soundbites and emojis and, when we can't face a real conversation, we send a text. I once got dumped that way and not after a casual fling.

They ended a long-term relationship with a short message. I mean who needs a heartfelt, honest conversation when you can hit send with a 'sorry, but we're over'.

Whenever we feel uneasy or insecure, we instinctively try to protect ourselves, doing whatever makes sense in the moment to feel safe and resolve our insecurities.

Habitual safety strategies take over, including:

- Dominating and controlling
- Ignoring, withdrawing, or keeping an emotional distance
- Staying quiet instead of speaking up
- Seeking reassurance, validation and approval
- Over-preparing and second guessing
- Delaying, distracting and deflecting
- Being defensive
- Blaming (either ourselves or others)
- Denying and minimising

These often unconscious safety behaviours can provide temporary comfort or a sense of control but, ultimately, they create more interference, not less. For example, if we don't express our true thoughts and feelings, resentment builds up, and with it comes a loss of compassion. We end up in a messy feedback loop that causes more misunderstanding. Not only do our relationships suffer but all that pretence, posturing and overthinking takes its toll on our mental well-being.

Insecurity feedback loop

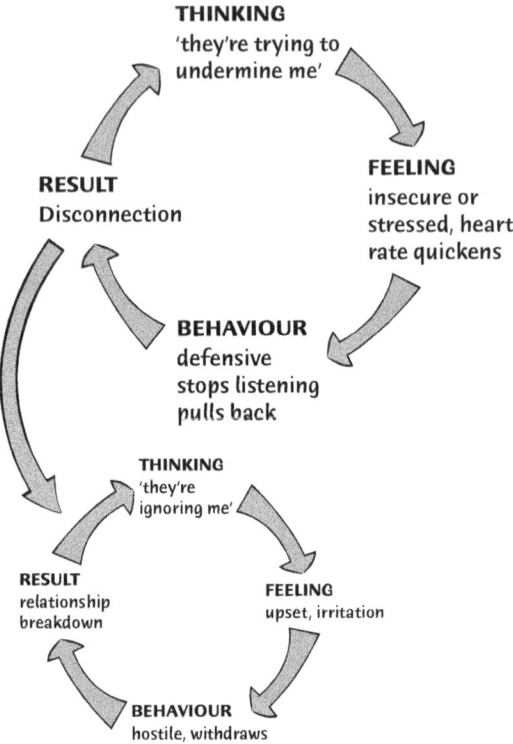

When I ask people what stops them from having honest conversations they typically say:

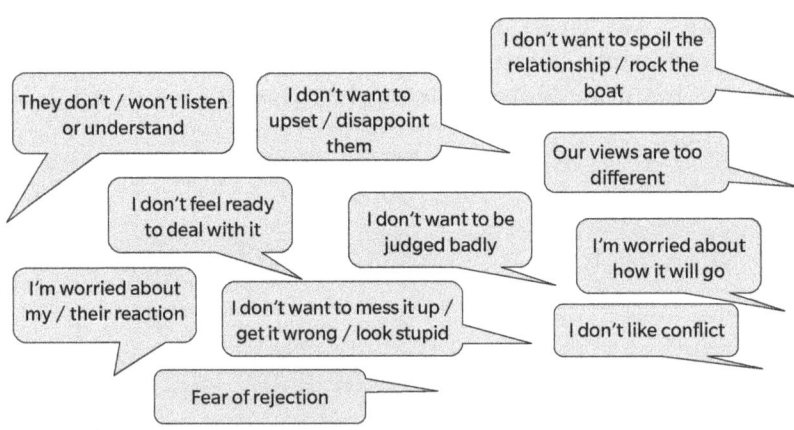

When it comes to relationships, the outside<in illusion creates patterns of thinking and behaviour that hijack our common sense and compassion.

Having honest, heartfelt conversations – the foundation of resilient relationships – is much easier when unnecessary noise is removed. Let's explore some of these pesky thought traps starting with my personal Achilles heel.

The responsibility trap

Many parents feel the weight of responsibility for their children's success or happiness. Managers feel the weight of responsibility for their team's results or motivation. Therapists might feel in some way responsible for their client's recovery. I've fallen into that trap a few times.

Let's imagine a friend is depressed and you want to help them feel better. Your well-intentioned desire to alleviate their suffering might create unwarranted anxiety or overwhelm as you try to shoulder a burden that isn't yours to bear. Then, when people don't respond as we hope or expect, we feel guilty, resentful or disappointed, as if we've failed in some way. And now it's become about us.

A friend shared this story with me about her boyfriend . . .

> 'Steve's elderly mother moved in with him after she fell and broke her hip. He's assumed responsibility for all her needs, including her happiness. His own needs are forgotten. He won't let himself relax or have fun. It's a full-time job tending to her physical and emotional well-being, so when his efforts aren't successful, he gets frustrated and resentful. And he can't see a way through, given that she's not going to

get any better and won't be able to live by herself. He often feels stressed and depressed.

'What's tricky about this situation is that, to Steve, it looks like he's being a good son in a difficult set of circumstances. He's obliged to do this because she's his mother after all. Yes, this is a heavy burden, he tells me, but that's life.

'I mistakenly thought that his sense of obligation was the cause of his stress. And that's tricky because he's committed to being her caregiver. But as I talked with a colleague, I realised it was extremely simple. It isn't possible to make another person happy or unhappy at will. So they are caught in this exhausting loop. He desperately tries to make her happy. She's crabby about her loss of independence, and he gets upset that she doesn't appreciate all he's doing for her.

'When you outsource your emotional well-being to someone or something, there's no limit to what you must do or deal with to make yourself and the people you love feel better. But her happiness comes from within, so no amount of attention and care from Steve is going to change anything unless something first changes in her way of seeing the world. And that's the conversation I wanted to have with Steve. No judgement. No right or wrong. Just how it works and how it doesn't work.'

Maybe you can relate in some way? When you think about your own relationships, do you ever feel a sense of responsibility for someone's feelings or behaviour?

There's a well-worn phrase – 'You can bring a horse to water but you can't make it drink.' While I was writing this chapter, I began to recognise a major blind spot. Sometimes, my concern and desire to help, especially with family and friends, makes me pushy and controlling. It's for their benefit after all. And when people won't do what is best for them (according to me), I get frustrated and keep pushing ahead, trying to convince and cajole. I thought I was gently guiding them to the water's edge, inviting them to take a sip.

But what I see now is that, even though my intentions were coming from love, sometimes I was dragging them to the water and practically pushing their heads in.

I was putting so much energy into trying to make people change. It's exhausting!

The Responsibility trap is made up of two false assumptions:

- I can control how you feel and behave by my words/feelings/actions.
- You can control how I feel and behave by your words/feelings/actions.

Steve's story is a great example of what can happen when both parties are caught in this trap.

How many times have you tried to stop someone from worrying needlessly or tried to get them to change because you knew it would help them but, despite your best efforts, it didn't work?

For years I tried to make my stepdad stop smoking. I shared research about the worst effects, plus the health benefits of quitting. I gifted him the much-celebrated Alan Carr book which my friend insisted was a game changer. He didn't listen to or read any of it. The only change was my growing frustration that he was still puffing 20 a day despite knowing it might end his marriage or kill him. Many months later, he did stop but he couldn't explain how or why. He said he woke up one morning and just knew that he didn't want to smoke anymore.

During a period where I'd piled on the pounds and having spent most of her life on a diet, my lovely Mum decided to help me lose weight. She tried the softly softly approach with a nudge here and there.

Then she moved onto the shaming strategy. You know, the one where they give you that look of disappointment where no words are needed. And when that didn't work, she put pen to paper and posted a kind and straight talking handwritten note to my home. Whatever response my Mum was expecting, ignoring her note probably wasn't one of them. Her tactics were well-meaning, but they were no match for my emotional eating and stubborn denial.

If we really had the power to change people at will, I would end prejudice and abuse and make everyone care more about animals and the planet and less about 'stuff'. I would eradicate ego based insecurity so we can have a loving, peaceful world without war, oppression and our obsession with 'likes'. And I would also make my partner less of a know it all ☺ A girl can dream.

Real change comes from the inside>out through our own realisations. But if we believe we have the power to affect someone's life for the better, of course we're going to try and exert that power, like Rachel did by trying to keep everyone happy. Except that we cannot control how people think, feel and behave.

We must be on different planets!

We were watching comedian Jo Koy on Netflix and, while I was belly laughing, my stepdad could barely summon a smile. He didn't get why I found it so funny and I thought someone had stolen his sense of humour.

How many times have you discussed something you feel strongly about and been surprised, annoyed, or even outraged that they didn't share the same view as you?

Sometimes, it really seems like we're on different planets and, in a way, we are because we all live in our own world of *Thought*. That's why one person's hankering for a hug feels suffocating for someone else. And why one person's cute baby voice (yes mine) is another person's ick (an ex).

Life is constantly revealing how reality is an inside job.

A painful but illuminating lesson in this happened 25 years ago when a member of my team called me into a meeting to tell me she was leaving. We had an honest, heartfelt conversation. I asked if we could do anything to persuade her to change her mind. I knew she'd been feeling a bit insecure, so I reassured her that we believed in her potential and asked if she was willing to give it more time or explore other roles. She teared up so I did my best to comfort her.

Three hours later, I was hauled into HR. She'd made a complaint about my conduct. I was totally blindsided and felt betrayed. Her version could not have been more different to mine. It was like she was describing a completely different conversation. Talk about living in our own realities! I learned an important lesson (as a manager) which is to find out what kind of conversation you are walking into and if in any doubt, bring someone else in as a neutral observer.

During my interviews with Dr Marilyn Bowman about her resilience research, she shared a story about being rushed into hospital with a serious illness. While her mother was inconsolable in the corridor, thinking that Marilyn was going to die, she was in the room asking the doctors a hundred questions. She was so curious about her condition, and fear just wasn't a factor. It was an early lesson for her about how we perceive life events so differently from each other.

We all have our own ideas, beliefs and values, whether it's politics, religion or something else. It's natural to want people to see things from your perspective, to acknowledge your views or jump on board with your ideas.

It's also easy to fall into the trap of assuming that people should think like you or that you should think like them and that, if we don't, there's something wrong. But we're designed to experience the world through our own subjective *Thought* lens. It cannot be any other way.

When we innocently forget that this is how it works, it leads to controlling, combative or defensive behaviour. We might miss out on the richness and rewards of loving, learning and growing.

> **'If one can only see things according to one's own belief system, one is destined to become virtually deaf, dumb, and blind.'**
>
> **Robert Anton Wilson, American novelist**

As much as you might want, expect or believe it to be true, my green will never be your green. I can't have your thoughts or emotions and you can't have mine. And when you remember this, it creates a different kind of conversation. Instead of pushing our own opinion or agenda, making ourselves or others wrong or assuming we know better, the only thing that makes sense is to open your heart and build bridges of understanding. This has the power to transform our relationships and create a wiser, more compassionate world.

When we try to take responsibility for other people's thoughts and feelings, it has some profound implications.

1. Impact on ourselves:

We might avoid being honest for fear of how it might land. This habitual care taking of other people's feelings can lead to resentment, anxiety or burnout because we're not being true to ourselves or taking care of our own needs.

Ask yourself:

What assumptions am I making? What am I telling myself that is stopping me from speaking up / starting the conversation?

2. Impact on others:

Helping people, whoever they are, requires permission, otherwise we might overstep boundaries. I didn't ask my stepdad if he wanted my help to stop smoking, and guess what, it wasn't well received.

Ask yourself:

Do I have permission, or I am just assuming they want my help?

Am I being in service to them or am I making this about me?

We might be dismissing or demonising feelings that need to be felt and processed.

In situations where we aren't comfortable with someone else's thoughts and emotions, we might try to change them to make ourselves feel better. For example, you might try to get someone to 'think more positively' because you're uncomfortable about them feeling upset.

Ask yourself:

Can I be okay with whatever thoughts and feelings another person might be having?

Am I trying to change how they feel because of how I think it makes me feel?

We might innocently project or reinforce the idea that a person lacks wisdom, or that they don't have as much resilience as others. For someone who already feels insecure and believes that other people are responsible for their feelings, this can lead to a sense of helplessness.

Signs of learned helplessness include:

Giving in/Giving up: When faced with obstacles that we *can* overcome, we might give up too soon. Like fleas trapped in a jar, when the lid comes off they stop trying to get out because they're now conditioned by a false limitation.

Being passive: We might not take action to address or change our situation for the better because we've become accustomed to someone else taking the lead. We might avoid taking accountability and end up relying on someone else to do our thinking for us.

Mental health issues: If we forget that we're designed with the inner resources to get through difficult times, we might feel helpless, inadequate or powerless, which can lead to anxiety or depression.

Ask yourself:

Do I know that everyone has resilience and wisdom, or am I seeing some people as broken or damaged in some way?

*When I'm in dialogue with people, am I thinking **for** them, instead of **with** them?*

How can I guide others to remember and reconnect with their innate resilience, without minimising their feelings or struggles?

If we want to empower positive change, we have to help each other realise and reconnect with our innate wholeness and resilience, instead of innocently reinforcing what is not and cannot be true.

'It's a relief to know that I'm not responsible for how people think and feel . . . I mean I still care. I still want them to be OK and I'm still here for them but now I know that their feelings are theirs, and mine are mine. I'm worrying a lot less and I think my relationships are actually better because of that,' Rachel shared.

The avoidance–attachment cycle

We've explored some of the implications when we think we're responsible for people's feelings or behaviour but what happens when you believe that other people can directly affect how you think and feel?

Jasmine wanted to talk with Steve about his sense of responsibility for his mum's happiness. She thought, if he could get a new perspective, he would feel less burdened and more relaxed, but she was holding back. I asked her why.

> **'I was afraid to mention it because he's very edgy about the whole situation, and we've already had arguments about her. Plus I hate conflict.**
>
> **'Growing up, there was no arguing at home. We were always trying to make sure my father didn't get upset because we didn't want him punching holes in walls. Also, I've seen Steve argue with his family and it's not pretty.'**

Jasmine had learned that keeping quiet at home helped to keep the peace. And this safety behaviour, which served her as a child, had followed her into adult life. When she's faced with the potential of someone she loves getting upset or angry, old memories surface and old habits kick in, which bring feelings of fear that stop her speaking up.

It's logical that if we are struggling with feelings of insecurity and we also believe those feelings come from how someone else thinks or behaves, we're going to respond in a way that protects us from being made to feel a way that we don't want to feel.[1] That could mean physically avoiding people or keeping some emotional distance. Intimacy and connection naturally get affected.

By ignoring or denying stuff that's important to deal with, resentment can build up. Then we get preoccupied with all the things we wanted to say and our minds get distracted and busy. We also miss the chance to deepen our relationships through honest conversations.

Your mood is yours; my mood is mine

Lucy wanted to be less defensive and more open when people had feedback or suggestions that she didn't necessarily want to hear. Interestingly, 61% of respondents to our research said they often or always get defensive and take things personally.[2]

She agreed to do an experiment for a couple of weeks to become more aware of her reactions without judging or analysing. When we met up again I asked what she had noticed.

> **'I was feeling upset one evening. Then it hit me that it can't be other people because I was at home alone. I even had my mood light on! I suddenly realised why I felt so crappy. I'd been ruminating for ages on a conversation from last week.'**

Lucy began to listen without getting into a reaction or making it about her. Conversations changed dramatically as her compassion and understanding for herself and others increased.

We can only be responsible for our own emotional state and behaviour. Knowing this, we are free from the effort of trying to control the uncontrollable.

Emily Atack, a British comedian, was sexually harassed online with threats of rape and graphic unsolicited images on a daily basis.[3] She was holding back from talking to her mum because she thought it would be too upsetting for her. 'I appreciate that you don't tell me about it all the time because I would be a wreck,' she tells Emily. They were both caught in the Responsibility trap.

There's a common saying, 'A problem shared, is a problem halved.' My partner often jokes that a problem shared is a problem doubled ☺ And there is truth in what he says. We can innocently take on the pain of another and internalise it, so it becomes our pain. When this impacts us in a negative way, it's described as compassion fatigue.

Compassion is a natural response when we see the struggles of others. Being able to witness another person's pain gives us a window into their reality but remember it is *their* reality. It is *their* pain, not yours.

We can love and care for each other, but we can't force feed joy or take away people's distress, much as we might want to. And, in some ways, this is good news because when you know how your mind works, it makes you more immune to manipulation and coercion. Fear and insecurity are one of the main reasons people stay in abusive relationships. We begin to doubt ourselves and this gets intensified when we think that someone else is responsible for our self-worth because they might intentionally play on your insecurities.

But what happens when we put the responsibility for our feelings onto others? When we think someone is the source of our joy, love, happiness, self-esteem, excitement etc, we might become attached to their presence, expecting them to fulfil all our emotional needs and desires.

Rachel thinks her happiness is dependent on other people's happiness. When people she loves are struggling, she feels compelled to try and make them feel better, not just for them, but for her own well-being. Her 'when-then' Thought trap is "'when you're ok, I'm ok'". But this divorces her from reality, creating a false dependency.

Ask yourself:

Do I think that other people need to think, feel or act in a particular way for me to be OK?

If you say I'm OK, then I must be OK

Relying on validation from someone else because you think it makes you feel emotionally secure can create an attachment to their approval. Not only does this disempower you but it puts an emotional burden on them as they try to provide something that they can't give you because it's already within.

When you remember that all feelings and perceptions are energy moving through you, you stop blaming or trying to get validation from others. You stop thinking that someone else needs to change for you to feel whole and complete. This frees your mind and liberates your relationships.

The Responsibility Trap

	Outside<in illusion	Inside>out reality
	The belief that something other than the power of *Mind* – including other people's thoughts, feelings or behaviour – could be responsible for your moment-to-moment emotions, perceptions or behaviour.	We live in a world that can only exist via the mind. All thoughts, feelings, perceptions and behaviour originate from *Mind* via *Thought and Consciousness*.

Indicators and implications	Outside<in illusion	Inside>out reality
Indicators and implications	You believe that people can cause you to feel a way you don't want to feel. This creates insecurity. Your well-being might feel threatened or you feel more vulnerable. You believe that people can make you feel a way you *do* want to feel, i.e. happy, content, capable, secure or confident. This can create a false sense of need and, at the extreme, over-reliance and co-dependency.	You recognise that other people are not responsible for your feelings. This means you don't rely on them for your peace of mind or self-worth. And it makes no sense to blame them for how you feel. Relationships are healthier. You feel naturally empowered. You feel psychologically safe and free.
Indicators and implications	You believe you can make someone feel a way they do or don't want to feel. It creates an illusory perception of control or responsibility. This misperception creates insecurity, worry, guilt or tension. It creates avoidance, defensiveness, dishonesty, detachment and controlling behaviour.	We can only feel what we think in each moment, not what someone else thinks. The subtraction of this outside<in interference removes tension, blame, guilt and resentment and leads to deeper trust, connection and compassion. You can be honest and speak your mind. You can handle the truth. You feel empowered and resilient.

Indicators and implications	Outside<in illusion	Inside>out reality
	You think people need to change their thoughts, feelings or behaviour for you to feel resilient or secure.	You know that no one needs to change for you to be OK.
	This belief leads to controlling, defensive or insecure thoughts, feelings and behaviour as you try to manage or avoid others, so that you can feel better.	You appreciate that people's behaviour reflects *their* current beliefs and state of consciousness. This leads to more empathy, compassion, curiosity and understanding.
		Note: this does not mean accepting behaviour that you feel is unacceptable, toxic or dangerous.

The knowledge trap

'I don't propose that it is a virtue to revel in our limitations. But it's important to understand how much we do not know.'

Carl Sagan

How many times have you been in a conversation, and thought to yourself, 'I know where this is going . . . '? Or you rehearse a future conversation in your head, where you play yourself *and* the other person?

I can be chatting with my partner one minute and the next he is literally walking away while I'm still speaking. 'Where are you going?' and 'Are you listening?' have been two recurring questions in my home.

Turns out he thought he already knew what I was going to say and therefore his presence was no longer required! Rude! Just between you and me, sometimes I drift off when he's telling me something, but at least I stay in the room.

The Knowledge trap is made up of three false assumptions:

- *I know what you're going to think, feel or do.*
- *I know what I am going to feel, think or do.*
- *I/you should know what I am going to feel, think or do.*

When we over-estimate the emotional impact of future events on our happiness or well-being, it's been named 'affective forecasting error'. For instance, someone might believe that winning the lottery will make them far happier but research that tracks jackpot winners has shown time and time again that their initial dopamine-fuelled high wears off quite fast and they return to their pre-lottery levels of happiness.

During a session with Anna, a self-confessed overthinker, she was telling me about a conversation she'd been dreading. "I used to spend so much time worrying about future situations and what other people might be thinking. I can't believe how much energy this has been taking from me. I was completely stressed during those four days, screaming at my kids, and it was totally unnecessary."

Often, when we think we're pre-empting or forward planning, what we're really doing is worrying. And they're not the same thing ☺

Useful distinction:
planning vs worring

Planning: thinking through what matters, assessing risks, scenario planning, considering viable options, breaking down complex tasks into manageable chunks. It's about being as prepared as possible, while knowing there are many unknowns, and we can adapt and respond in the moment to whatever shows up.

Worrying: ruminating or agonising about what could/should/might happen and trying to pre-empt every possible scenario or outcome. Thinking we know what the future holds and living in a fear-based story. Thinking that our fundamental well-being or resilience is somehow at the mercy of some future outcome. It becomes a self-perpetuating loop of concern.

Michelle had to make some redundancies at work and she was dreading it, thinking she would break their hearts or ruin people's lives. Time after time, they responded very differently to how she anticipated. She began to notice that her preparation for those conversations was based on how she thought she would feel in that situation. It was a projection of her own insecurities and imagined futures.

Thought experiment

What will you think in two minutes from now?

How will you feel tomorrow when you wake up?

How will you feel next Tuesday at 4pm?

If I knew what I was going to think next and was able to control my thinking, I would order less judgement, more compassion and genius ideas on a daily basis. I couldn't cope with hourly brilliance. Way too tiring.

Inside>out fact checker:

♥ We cannot know what we will think or feel in a future moment. Only that we *will* think and feel in every moment that we're alive.

♥ We cannot know what someone else will think and feel in some future moment. Only that they *will* think and feel in every moment that they're alive.

♥ We cannot know what insights, ideas or realisations will come to mind. Only that insights, ideas and realisations *will* come to mind.

But when we think we know, it shows up in our conversations as:

overthinking and worry . . . false expectations . . . shallow listening . . . lack of flexibility . . . hijacking . . . dominating . . . holding back . . . second guessing, etc.

Jasmine thought she knew what would happen if she talked to Steve, including how it would make her feel (crappy) so she stopped herself speaking up.

When we assume we know how someone else will think or feel it can lead to misunderstandings and miscommunication. Assumptions can stop us listening and our lack of curiosity can send the message that we're not interested in how someone is feeling, even when this isn't our intention. We miss the chance to connect and understand their reality.

The only way to escape this trap, is to remember that we *don't know.*

Life is unfolding thought by thought, moment to moment. The future is at best a projection, a forecast, a story that we create. But this isn't saying don't think ahead. It's helpful to consider what we want to communicate or what might be important to the other person or what outcome you might want.

But, ultimately, we have no idea what will occur *in the moment*. We have no idea what insights will ignite. This means that whenever you envisage a future conversation, you are always experiencing the Products of *Thought* right now. Any forecast of the future, however compelling or logical, is always incomplete.

You can never know how you will respond until that moment comes. This being true, it gives you a practical reason to be less attached to thinking about the past or future. Instead you can let conversations unfold naturally, in the present moment, because that's where the action and the magic is. Now is all we have.

When Michelle imagined what people would think and feel when she told them their job was coming to an end, what she was doing – innocently – was disregarding or forgetting that;

Every human being has the capacity for insight.

Every human being is innately resilient and wise.

We can never truly know what is right or possible for another person (or for ourselves).

Being open to the present moment and the power of insight can help us to have deeper and more productive dialogue. It allows us to listen and learn from each other and build trust, which leads to stronger relationships and more positive outcomes.

The Knowledge Trap

	Outside<in illusion	Inside>out reality
	We think we know how we will think, feel or behave in some future moment. We think we know what will happen in a future moment.	We cannot know what thoughts, feelings and subsequent behaviour will occur in any future moment. The future is at best a projection, forecast or story that the mind creates. We can only experience reality now based on how the Principle of *Thought* is unfolding and taking form in each moment.
Indicators and implications	You worry about how you will feel in the future. These feelings seem to legitimise your concerns, fuelling further concern, creating a feedback loop of insecurity.	Knowing that it's not possible to know what will occur in a future moment, your mind is unburdened and you're more available in the present. You feel psychologically secure. You can listen more deeply.
Indicators and implications	You think you know how someone is going to think or feel in a future moment. You try to pre-empt or make assumptions and judgements about how they might react.	Knowing that you cannot know how someone will think and feel in a future moment, it doesn't make sense to overthink or try to second guess all the possible scenarios. This leaves your mind free of unnecessary worry. You can listen and respond in the moment.

➤

Indicators and implications	Outside<in illusion	Inside>out reality
	You think you know what other people are thinking or feeling. You become a mind-reader. You mistake this for empathy. You make assumptions and fill in the gaps. You're not listening. You're not present.	You recognise you can never know or directly feel what another thinks and feels. We are always perceiving the world through own subjective thought system.
		This recognition encourages neutrality , compassion and curiosity in how you listen. You connect more deeply. There's more openness and trust.
Indicators and implications	You think other people should know what you are thinking and feeling. You get dismayed or upset when they don't.	It's not possible for someone to know what you are thinking or feeling however intuitive or connected you feel. It makes no sense to expect someone to know without sharing and helping each other to understand each other's reality understand our reality.

The expectation trap

A friend shared this story.

"When Rich and I were first married, I did what I thought wives were supposed to do. Every night I made dinner so it was ready for him. Growing up, we had dinner at 6pm every night when my Dad got home. Even though Mum worked too, there was an expectation that dinner would be on the table. My husband was the opposite. He got home later and wanted to have a drink, listen to music and relax. I would be hungry and furious. I just thought he was ungrateful. I expected him to appreciate my efforts. Every time he got home, I was pissed off. Who could blame him for not wanting to rush back? This went on for months, until we talked it through."

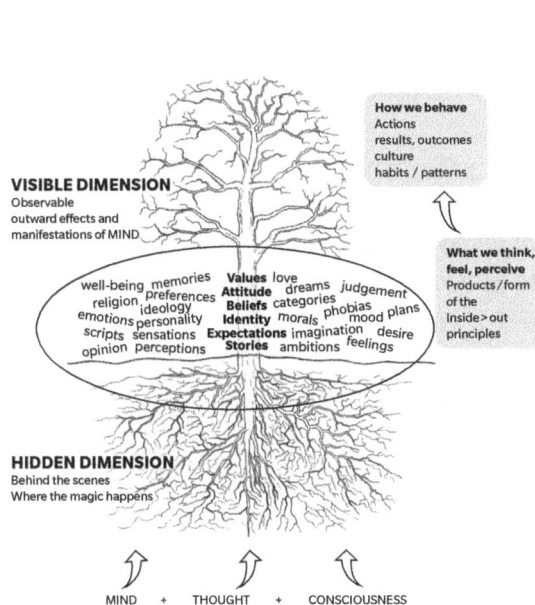

We've all got preferences, pet peeves, beliefs, rules, values or ideas that we hold dear. We have all kinds of opinions about how life should be, or how others should behave.

And these perceptions become unspoken expectations and requirements that we carry into our conversations and relationships, often without realising.

Then we assess and attach our sense of satisfaction, compatibility, and opinions of others, on how well they meet our expectations or standards.

Most of the time we don't even know what each other's expectations are, either because they're not visible, or because we haven't shared them. We just expect people to know ☺.

Think about a specific relationship that you want to improve, or a conversation that you're due to have. It could be with a romantic partner, a family member, a friend, client or co-worker.

Ask yourself:

What am I expecting from this conversation, person or relationship?

What do I think they are expecting from me?

In what ways could my expectations and assumptions be creating unnecessary interference, barriers or disconnection?

How open am I being to new perspectives that challenge my thinking?

What are the possibilities for connection, understanding and progress when I remember that my preferences and expectations are Thought and not facts?

There's nothing wrong with having expectations but when we identify with them as if they're fixed and we forget they are made up, it creates unwarranted limitations and barriers in relationships. It stops us hearing each other. It curtails our compassion. It impacts how we approach everything in life. This includes persistent complaints that keep you from connecting with and enjoying what and who you have in front of you.

The identity trap

I experience you as a reflection of how I see myself. You experience me as a reflection of how you see yourself. There is no getting away from this.

Our attachment to ego or self-image dominates our interactions. It keeps us thinking that we are separate from each other.

> **'Ego is everything we think we are and everything we think about life.'**
>
> **Syd Banks**

Racism and prejudice are symptoms of the trap of knowledge *and* identity. It's a function of becoming attached to our ideas of who we think people are.

We judge people based on their religious beliefs (or our own). We judge people based on perceived ability or disability. We make assumptions based on someone's age. We dismiss people based on their cultural background or heritage. We discriminate based on superficial differences.

> **'A great many people think they are thinking, when they are merely rearranging their prejudices.'**
>
> **William James, psychologist and author**

Every time you wish someone would change or be different, what you're doing is wanting them to meet your expectations of who you think they are or should be. But who you think they are doesn't exist. All that exists is your story.

It's easy to believe that our perceptions of people are reality. But we never see people as they truly are. We see and experience them as a reflection of our own consciousness.

Our listening is full of beliefs, stories and personal history. We can't stop that from happening, but we can recognise *that* it's happening.

What if we could see people without our pre-conceptions and judgements in the way?

'To understand relationship, you must understand yourself and the whole process of "I" and "you".'

Jiddhu Krishnamurti

When we recognise that what we think has nothing to do with the essence of someone, a space opens for deeper connection and we can begin to really know and understand each other beyond our personal beliefs, stories and neurosis.

Our ego thinking wants to be validated and reassured. It wants to be accepted. It wants to be right. We're so desperate to avoid feelings of shame, embarrassment, shyness or inadequacy, that we pretend, avoid, lie and diminish ourselves or others.

It always comes back to feelings . . . having them, stopping them, keeping them.

A workplace study in 2003 found that 85% of participants didn't want to approach their manager with work concerns because they were worried about being perceived in a negative light.[4] Our preoccupation with what others think of us is a common trap. We want to belong, to be accepted and loved. And any time we think this is under threat, we default to protecting ourselves.

When I was younger, my concern with being liked was so all-consuming that I curated my words and actions to make myself fit what I believed people wanted me to be. But you cannot know or control what someone else thinks and feels about you. And, more importantly, what someone thinks and feels about you has no power, other than the power we give it with our own minds. I wish I had known this back then.

As spiritual teacher Byron Katie says; 'It's not your job to like me – it's my job.'[5]

The Identity Trap

IDENTITY	Outside<in illusion	Inside>out reality
	The belief that there is a separate 'I'/'me'/'self' with a fixed or pre-determined identity. When we don't include Mind as the creator of self.	Everything we think about ourselves, other people and the world, is a creation of mind. There is no 'self' outside of the realm of con-sciousness. We think ourselves into being.
Indicators and Implications	You believe that there is a self-image you must pro-tect, validate and live up to. You think this image/concept is the totality of who you are. This creates defensive and protection-ist behaviour.	You realise there is no fixed identity to protect or live up to. All ideas of 'I/me' are products of the Principle of *Thought* in different disguises that you've been perceiving as real/true. You feel a connection to a deeper or greater sense of 'self' beyond the personal.
Indicators and Implications	You label and judge people and then relate to them through that thought lens as if it were reality. You believe your perceptions of them (ideas, beliefs, expecta-tions) are who they are.	You appreciate that your perceptions of people aren't who they are but just how the mind is perceiving them. This rec-ognition helps you to see people's true potential. You have more awareness of your own biases and pre-conceptions.

Indicators and Implications	Outside<in illusion	Inside>out reality
	You think you need other people's approval to validate your existence or value. You think you need to be liked to feel OK. Other people have the power to give or take away your sense of worth, contentment, well-being and resilience.	You know that how you feel about yourself is a function of *Thought* in the moment and, ultimately, cannot be determined by anyone or anything. You sense a deeper value and worth that is beyond your past, your stories and anything you can think about yourself. In the light of this knowledge, you feel unconditionally empowered and secure.
Indicators and Implications	You take criticism or feedback as a 'personal attack'. For example, a 'no' feels like rejection of you as a person. This generates self-conscious, reactive, defensive or judgemental behaviour.	You recognise it's not about you. Everyone is living from their own subjective realities. It's never personal. It just feels personal. On seeing this, you're able to relate to people and situations less defensively, with more neutrality and compassion.

A clearing for hearing

How we think about the world becomes a filter that colours and shapes our listening. We bring our past into the present and then project it into the future.

Imagine being in a conversation where you are concerned about your self-image, worried about saying the wrong thing, you think the other person is responsible for how you feel and you think you know how it's all going to play out. This is the kind of outside-in noise we bring to our conversations. It's a miracle that we manage to have any decent conversations.

I have this long-standing joke with a friend of mine where I say 'have a nice day', and he replies 'Don't tell me what to do!'

What we say and how someone hears it are two different things and you don't get to control that.

Diversity is a natural and inevitable result of operating through our own subjective thinking in each moment. It's the nature of being human. And conflict is the experience of different perspectives colliding.

If you factor this in, that's enough to navigate conversations more wisely. And when there's misunderstanding, you can listen with more neutrality, without taking it personally.

But what happens when we so disagree so fundamentally with someone's perspective, that we cannot bring ourselves to even begin a conversation?

An absence of love is a call for love

Deeyah Khan is an award-winning documentary maker who also happens to be Muslim. On a podcast with Simon Sinek, she talks about spending time with white supremacists as she tries to get a deeper understanding of their beliefs and behaviour.

> **'I'm actually always looking for the light, I'm actually always looking for the love, I'm looking for the cracks where some level of humanity might reside. So the entire process of making the films is trying to understand the darkness.'[6]**

Given that reality is an inside job, everyone is going to have their own logic for what they believe and how they behave. Even when it seems a million miles from how you see the world. And even it seems completely abhorrent to you.

Deeyah explains:

> '**Everyone's this sort of hero in their own head. And
> most people who do awful things, in their mind don't
> think that they're doing awful things. They think
> they're actually doing the right thing. They actually
> think they're doing the righteous thing.**'

We are all projecting our insecurities and neuroses onto each other,
judging and blaming and expecting the other person to fix it.

Something that Deeyah said struck me.

> '**I have sat with some of the worst of the worst, quote
> unquote, people . . . people who've done horrific things,
> convicted terrorists, all sorts of people. And really, it all
> always comes back to love. And the second they sense
> any feeling that even resembles that from you they are
> willing to sit there in that discomfort with you. They are
> willing to sit there and put their entire life in your hands.
> I mean, I've sat with some of these guys and some of the
> things that they've shared with me [............] . . . even
> I have sat there going, you really shouldn't tell me
> this, you know, because whatever I don't know I can't
> include so don't . . . they're like, no, I trust you. And so
> without love, truly there is nothing.**'

When our conversations are about winning, being right, making
someone else wrong or scoring points, then it's a conversation led by
insecurity. There is no real listening or compassion present.

We all want to be heard and seen without judgement. In that way,
listening *is* love. It's the simple act of really being with another
human being. And this is far easier to do when we catch on to what's
getting in the way.

Loving connection is always available when we see beyond our superficial and conditioned thinking to the core of our shared humanity.

The Myth of Panic

This myth has been well researched and written about. It's based on the belief that when presented with 'bad news', people will overreact, behave erratically and somehow lose their capacity to function out of fear.

If we buy into this belief, we become more pre-occupied with pre-empting and worrying about people's reactions, than we do about dealing with the real-world risk and implications of the situation at hand. The consequences of this fear of fear, is often more damaging than any risk attached to telling the truth.

We're seeing this in the current downplaying of the ecological crisis and the widespread denial of how serious it is. Rather than do the right thing, many of our political leaders are opting for the popular route or the path of least resistance. But history shows us that in the face of difficult truths and genuine crisis, people pull together, support their communities, find solutions and adapt fast. Panic is not the typical response.

You can handle the truth; *we* can handle the truth

How many times have you held back from sharing something because you thought someone couldn't handle the truth? Or maybe you've stuck your fingers in your ears because you thought you couldn't handle hearing something.

Everyone is innately resilient at their core. We all have a well of wisdom and common sense. When we remember and honour this in each other, we won't feel the need to shield or protect each other's feelings. All that avoidance, analysing and worrying is removed.

There might be times when we need to be more cautious or careful with how we communicate – particularly with those who are more vulnerable. But honesty isn't something we should be compromising.

In a radio interview, a counsellor described interviewing a young person about the climate emergency. The counsellor said, 'How should we talk with young people like you about this? What advice would you give adults?'

The child said, 'Tell me the truth. Because if I find out you didn't then I won't be able to trust you. And if I can't trust you, I won't listen to you.' They added, 'And anyway, I'm not stupid.'

As adults we can learn so much from the wisdom of children.

Beyond forgiveness

Some people live with resentment, guilt or ill feeling towards others, sometimes for many years.

When my sister and I were young children, my dad had an affair, stole my Mum's jewellery and left the family home to move, quite literally, to the other side of the world. As birthdays came and went with zero contact, my sister and I grew resentful. In my late twenties, I attended a seminar where they suggested that forgiveness was the key to resolving hurt and finding peace of mind. They invited us to write a letter to the person we needed to forgive so we could get closure. I wrote one but it didn't help.

In my early 30s, after my Dad suffered a stroke, I flew with a friend to South Africa where he was living. I knew it might be the last time I would see him. Despite his frail condition, I still wanted answers but nothing he said could justify his earlier decisions and behaviour. And nothing could soften my feelings of hurt.

Fast forward to 2011. I'm in Santa Clara County in the USA visiting a maximum-security jail with friend and mentor Cathy Casey, where she's teaching some classes.

'If they're wearing orange trousers, they've done some pretty bad stuff,' Cathy says as we enter the building. I hear another set of iron gates lock behind me. The sign on the wall says something to the effect of 'You're entering at your own risk'. Great! That's reassuring, I think to myself as I walk into a room of bright orange trousers.

'Who wants to share something today?' Cathy asks the group. Joe's hand goes up: 'The reason I'm here, doing life, is because I believed my thinking and acted on it.'

As I listen to Joe's story, I'm moved to tears. He tells us that, on his first day in prison, he sees the doctor. Standard. He gets diagnosed with several mental health issues and prescribed several drugs. Apparently, this is also standard practice in these environments. After attending some of Cathy's classes, Joe tells us that he had an epiphany.

'I called my wife. I said "There's nothing wrong with me, I don't need the meds anymore. I'm healthy."'

He goes on to explain how the doctor had judged him based on how he was presenting on that specific day, together with Joe's personal history, including the crimes, evaluation notes from staff, etc. But he now understands that his thinking and his past are not who he is. They're not his true identity. He realised that behind all the fear and anger is an untouchable, spiritual core of common sense and love that can never be taken away.

I was so touched by what he shared. And then later it hit me like a ton of bricks. My dad believed his insecure thinking and acted on it. It wasn't an absence of love. It was a tsunami of insecurity. And then I remembered that, while I sat at his bedside, he shared many regrets with me – none of which I had been able to hear until this moment, sitting in Santa Clara County Jail, in the last place I expected to find healing.

If my dad had felt or known different, he would have done different. And while it didn't excuse the choices he made, I could appreciate that, if I had lived in his mind, had his thinking, felt his feelings, then who knows what decisions I might have made. Like every person on the planet, he was living from his own subjective reality, moment to moment, day to day.

He hadn't intentionally set out to hurt us. He felt insecure about his place in the world, so he did what made sense to resolve those feelings. Fear was in the driving seat, making all the decisions.

As the truth of this dawned on me, years of bad feeling vanished. I felt full of compassion and understanding. The resentment and contempt was gone. I finally found peace with the past.

I also knew that, if I had been able to really 'see' and hear him, I would have realised all of this while I was with him. I felt some regret that I couldn't bring that compassion to our last moments, but we can't give what we don't think and feel.

For years, I believed closure meant forgiving, but this isn't true. All we need is some love and understanding, which for me happened as soon as I glimpsed the truth of the situation, beyond my story.

'Why struggle to open a door between us when the whole wall is an illusion?'

Rumi, Persian poet, Sufi mystic

We don't need special rapport strategies or listening skills. True connection is that deep sense of love and kinship that we experience when we are really *with* another being and not inside our own heads.

Everyone is responding to their relationship with the mental activity that dominates their consciousness in each moment. This is the dominant relationship in our lives and the one we most need to understand.

The myth of separation

It was 1995 and I was attending a relationship seminar. 'Look at the person next to you. Where do you end and they begin?' the speaker asked us. 'If we could perceive people as they really are, there would be no separation . . . no division at all.'

To our limited human senses, it looks and feels like we are individual beings – and we are in terms of how we use *Thought* to make meaning and personalise life.

But like snowflakes, we are manifestations of a single source of energy in billions of different forms, with individual mind-made realities.

Back then, I believed oneness was woo-woo but I was wrong. Oneness is the essence of life. We're all connected at the deepest level. Every species on the planet. We are each made of the same stuff of the universe.

> **'We are like islands in the sea, separate on the surface but connected in the deep.'**
>
> **William James**

In essence

- -

- ♥ Conversations are not difficult nor easy. How we feel about them is a matter of perception, not fact.

- ♥ We don't have to force rapport and connection – we just need to uncover it by getting out of the way.

- ♥ Disagreement/different perspectives are the true nature of being human – because we each live from our own subjective realities.

- ♥ Empathy is a natural by-product of understanding separate realities.

- ♥ Presence, love and connection is our natural state of being.

- ♥ We are all connected. At our essence, there is no separation. We are one.

Bonus chapter materials here: http://www.chantalburns
.com/bulletproof-chapter-7-courageous-conversations-resilient-
relationships

chapter 8

Grief, loss and the true healer

'If you want to hold yourself and your family members compassionately through grief, you have to allow that it cannot be managed.'

Elizabeth Gilbert

On 4 October 2013, Khalil said goodnight to his children as he always did. The next morning, when he called for his son, there was no answer. Charlie had passed away in his sleep. He had no underlying conditions that his family knew of. He was 16 years old.

Nick's son Rory was 20 years old when he took his own life in the Summer of 2018. Although during his teens he had openly talked about ending his life, Nick felt that his son had turned a corner.

In early July 1998, having just lost the sight in his right eye, Giles got on a coach in Leeds. By the time he arrived in London four hours later, he had lost the sight in his left eye. Soon after that, he found himself bed bound, unable to walk.

Each of these people experienced profound loss, changing their lives forever.

In Nick's time of loss, he found himself on a spiritual path that took him by surprise . . . one that keeps him deeply connected with his son.

When Giles lost his eyesight, he lost his sense of identity and place. 'It was my first experience of grief because I was grieving for the person I was and for the person I thought I might become,' Giles told me. But he also found a surprising sense of freedom to recreate himself and his life.

For Khalil, losing his child led to a total dismantling of who he thought he was. It caused him to re-evaluate everything he thought was true. This journey, which at times has been beyond any suffering he has ever experienced, also led him to a place of peace that he hadn't thought was possible.

When life challenges us in ways we could never have imagined, we might begin to question everything we believed until that point. Some of us grieve for what could have been. Long-held dreams disappear overnight, leaving what can feel like a huge void. For some, that void feels scary. We lose a love we thought would last forever and some mourn the childhood they never had. For others, it might be the loss of physical or mental abilities.

In the same way that earthquakes create a seismic shift in the ground beneath our feet, there are circumstantial earthquakes. Sometimes sudden, other times forewarned, we encounter changes that tear apart the fabric of our lives.

While loss and death are inevitable, how we experience them is not a given. Loss can be full of suffering and, equally, it can be full of joy and unexpected gifts.

In some cultures, death is seen as a path to rebirth and enlightenment, bringing us back to our essence. Some regard death and loss as a rite of passage or a doorway to deeper feelings and connection.

The experience of loss reflects our own shifting perceptions and the meaning we are creating and projecting in each moment.

And, when we forget this, our minds will generate all kinds of justifications and assumptions for why and what we feel. This includes some persistent myths about loss and grieving. Even if you don't subscribe to these, new perspectives can support you in helping those who are struggling with loss.

Myth 1: There are specific stages for grieving

Psychiatrist Elizabeth Kubler-Ross interviewed people who were in the final moments of their lives. She observed a range of emotions and behaviour that she named denial, anger, bargaining, depression, acceptance. They became known as 'The Five Stages of Grief'. I first came across this concept in my consulting work. It's been adapted and widely used by organisations as a framework to help staff navigate change.

As Kubler-Ross was nearing the end of her own life, Oprah asked her if she had gone through these stages herself. She gave an emphatic 'No!' Followed by, 'I was angry, angry, angry.'[1] And when asked if there was denial, she said, 'Oh no, are you kidding? No denial, no bargaining . . . '

In another conversation with Oprah, Kubler-Ross famously said, 'Let's get past the stages. That's not the point of my work.' It turns out that she never intended her observations to be used in such a prescriptive way. But, like many ideas, 'The Five Stages of Grief' took on a life of its own and, while plenty of professionals no longer refer to it, the core premise is still popular in counselling, bereavement therapy and change management. The inside>out psychology explains why this concept has gained so much popularity.

When feelings of fear, sorrow, anger or distress become overwhelming, a framework or model like this one seems to bring comfort. It gives us something to hold on to when we feel like we're stranded at sea without a life jacket.

When someone says, 'You're going to feel like this, and then you'll feel like that,' it might bring a sense of order to the chaos. It normalises our emotions. It gives you a sense of certainty or security because you think, 'I know what's coming.' But we never do because we can never truly know what the next moment holds. All we can do is live our lives as best we can, one thought at a time, one moment at a time.

Facts versus ideas

When we get presented with a 'tried and tested' concept, we might relate to it as if it's fact. Especially if you don't remember that all models are made up. Just like the myth of personality, when we factualise something, this apparent fixedness gets reflected in how we think, feel and behave.

The assumption that there's a formula for grieving (or for any state of mind), creates mental interference including feelings of inadequacy, shame or blame. Our natural wisdom and clarity are drowned out by the noise of conditioned beliefs and biases.

For example, if your experience of loss doesn't match the next stage in the grief model you've learned about, you might judge yourself or others in some way.

There might be truth in a model, but the model isn't truth

Many of the emotions and behaviour that Kubler-Ross observed may well occur in times of loss but they are just as likely *not* to occur.

There's a big difference between *how something works* and *what sometimes happens*. Yet, as humans, we often confuse the two.

Useful distinction:
in the moment vs stages

Grief isn't a stage or a pre-determined journey. It's an *in the moment* state of consciousness. The experience of grieving is a dynamic, ever-changing flow of thought, feelings and sensations, shaping our behaviour. In one moment, we can be laughing and, in the next, crying or feeling hopeless. Our mind will move us from heaven to hell and back again in the blink of an eye.

You probably know from your own experience that grieving a loss doesn't follow a specific sequence or timeline. It's not a linear process. How could it be, when we don't know what the mind will manifest in the next moment?

Loss is happening through you, not to you.

In his book *The Other Side of Sadness*,[2] Professor George Bonanno says: 'Our feelings of emotion emerge as a kind of read out of what is going on in our mind at the moment.'

We're designed to experience a depth and range of feelings and emotions. That's a universal truth. And each person's loss will be profoundly personal to them because it's always happening from the inside>out. That too is a universal truth.

In times of deep sadness, I've found myself leaning into intense feelings and allowing space for them. When I was younger and had my first significant heart break, I closed my bedroom door and put on the saddest song I could find. Then I climbed into my bed, curled up in my duvet and cried as hard as I could until the snot ran down my face. After a while, with eyes red and swollen, I turned the music off, wiped my face, blew my nose, and got on with my day.

Looking back, I realise this was my way of handling heartache and dealing with those waves of emotion that engulfed me. Even before I understood anything about the mind, I didn't try to push those feelings away. I let myself fall into them fully, without struggle. There was something cathartic and healing about the tears and sadness.

There is nothing wrong with any feeling, however intense it may feel. As Kubler-Ross said during her conversation with Oprah:

'Just be you. If you feel like screaming, just scream. If you feel like crying you cry. Don't try to follow a textbook or have someone else tell you what to do.

Trust yourself . . . your own natural emotions.'

There is no right or wrong way to experience change or loss. There is just your way.

'Grief is a force of energy that cannot be controlled or predicted. It comes and goes on its own schedule. Grief does not obey your plans, or your wishes. Grief will do whatever it wants to you, whenever it wants to. In that regard, Grief has a lot in common with Love.'

Elizabeth Gilbert, journalist and novelist

This leads us to another misperception.

Myth 2: Distress is inevitable and necessary for grieving

There's an assumption that, if we're not showing distress in times of loss, there must be something wrong. For example, if we don't cry, it means that either we're not grieving, that we haven't accepted the reality of the situation, that we're reacting abnormally or supressing our feelings.

It's often assumed that sorrow, distress or even depression is somehow the correct way to respond to loss or adversity. There is no evidence to support the idea that a lack of distress (or other reactions) is abnormal or pathological. In fact, a deep dive into the available research reveals the opposite, as summed up by Bonanno and colleagues, when they said: 'Mild or absent grief reactions are not rare but tend to occur as often as, and sometimes more than any other response to loss.'[3]

This also relates to the belief that, if we're not tearful or troubled in response to death or loss, these emotions will inevitably rear their head in the future. This idea has been named 'prolonged grief' and is currently listed in the 'Diagnostic and Statistical Manual of Mental Disorders'.[4] By pathologising people's journey in this way, we are dismissing the natural diversity of spiritual and human experience.

Linked to this, one of the most common thought traps when it comes to grieving . . .

It's not OK to feel OK.

On the same day that Mary's father passed away, she went to meet some friends for a drink: 'In the pub I had a moment which I'll never forget when I was laughing and enjoying myself and thinking "that's so wrong". I felt so guilty about those feelings I was having because that wasn't supposed to be what was going on at that point in time.'

I asked Mary why she felt that way. She said, 'There are certain things you attach to grieving, which I wasn't doing. I wasn't doing the right things at that time because I thought, "No. That's not allowed, I should be crying. I shouldn't be going out. I should be upset. I should be all the stuff that people attach to a death."'

Like many who have lost loved ones, Mary believed there was a particular way she was meant to respond. And these thoughts were kept alive by some additional insecurity.

> **'I kept wondering what other people were thinking about me . . . being conscious of the fact that people might be thinking "Wow, her dad just died . . . what is she doing laughing in the pub, having a drink. How dare she! That's not what you do. Didn't she care about her dad?"'**

Mary's concerns about other people's thinking created an additional layer of mental interference, fuelling feelings of worry and shame but, as we've explored in previous chapters:

- We don't know what another person is thinking or feeling as we cannot think their thoughts and feel their feelings. We can only experience the power of *Thought* as it takes form within our own mind and body.

- What others may (or may not) be thinking or feeling, has no bearing on your wisdom, well-being or clarity, unless you think it does.

It's OK to feel OK

Chris, a graduate of my leadership school, went through some very challenging years where his young daughter had Leukaemia and his parents had major health issues. Because Chris had learned that his daughter's health was not responsible for his own feelings and behaviour, he was able to live with a depth of peace and well-being throughout some of the most challenging years of his life. During this period, what stood out most to him was other people's reactions.

'How are you able to function so well with all this going on?'; 'You must feel terrible'; 'It must be so hard'; 'How can you be so calm?'; 'I don't know how you are coping' were typical comments that Chris would get.

Whenever we interact with people, we are always projecting our own mental life (emotions, sensations, perceptions), without realising we are doing that.

For example, we hear about someone's loss, and it triggers a memory from the past.

Or we begin to imagine being in a similar scenario. As your imagination fires up, you experience a symphony of emotions, sensations and chemicals coursing through your system. In nano-seconds, your mind responds to those sensations and sometimes we share those thoughts and feelings, assuming they will be true for the other person.

'*You must [feel terrible]*' is really saying: '*When I think about what this would be like for me, I [feel terrible].*'

Or '*I think I would [feel terrible] if this happened to me.*'

You can add any feeling labels into those brackets.

Khalil shared something about this that struck me:

> **'How can I speak to somebody . . . how can I get solace . . . how can I derive some kind of contentment from the conversation, from somebody who sits opposite, that at best pities me?'**

Yes but . . . what about empathy? when you care about people and witness their suffering, surely it's natural for your heart to go out to them and to show them you understand.

There is a fine line between empathy and mindreading. As Aldous Huxley said:

> **'Nobody can actually feel another's pain or grief, another's love or joy or hunger. And similarly, nobody can experience another's understanding of a given event or situation.'**[5]

When I remember that I can only directly experience what's within my own consciousness, it stops making sense to try and guess how people are feeling or to expect someone to know how I am feeling. All I can do is get curious and ask.

As Khalil shared: 'If you're a clever person and you're quite empathetic and a good listener, you can make a pretty good stab at helping somebody articulate how they feel. But at best, you're helping that person articulate how *they* feel . . . you have no words to put into their mouths.'

To be present with someone . . . to really hear them and love them unconditionally . . . this is true empathy. And it's the only thing that makes sense when we remember we are each living out a holographic experience of our own consciousness.

Are you parking grief or avoiding grief?

In times of bereavement or loss, you might go into care taking mode. You might find yourself focusing on practical things that need attention. And yes, sometimes it will be a coping mechanism. We begin organising, planning or supporting other people. This could mean that we ignore or put aside our own thoughts and feelings. But it doesn't make it wrong or pathological. It doesn't mean that we're not grieving.

We do what makes sense to us in the moment, given the reality that our mind is manifesting.

It's true that denial can be a feature of bereavement. Sometimes, it's hard to come to terms with a loss. Sometimes, our thoughts or emotions may feel too painful to hang out with.

Caroline Flack was a popular and talented UK TV presenter. After more than one suicide attempt, she tragically took her own life in 2020. In a televised documentary, her mum said, 'She didn't handle heart break well,' and Caroline's twin sister Jody said, 'She really didn't think she could cope with that feeling.'[6] Caroline's attempts to take her own life were a desperate bid to control thoughts and feelings that she ultimately found too hard to live with.

Imagine the solace we could find in moments of distress if we whole-heartedly knew that those feelings were a passing state of mind, a flow of energy, and not something to fear. When we're not demonising ourselves and our feelings, suffering is reduced and we can't help but feel more settled during times of deep sorrow.

Myth 3: Grief needs acceptance and closure

Through my research into grief, the many people I've spoken with and my own experience, it's become clear that grief doesn't end. Instead, our sense of loss and the changes it brings become integrated into our lives. As a friend told me after losing her partner unexpectedly, 'I don't think you ever accept it. You just learn to live with it.'

We don't bounce back. We evolve.

As Khalil touched on: 'An awful lot of people talk about resilience as being able to bounce back. And I think that's missing the target. And it's actually missing the definition of what resilience is. It's not bouncing back. It's evolving and adapting to the situation that you found yourself in and finding a way forward. You don't bounce back because you're never the same person.'

Khalil realised that his life before Charlie's passing is now a part of his personal history.

> **'There was no rational reason for me to even spend one minute of my life contemplating how I can have back the life that I had. That was an impossibility . . . that's never on the cards, is it? You're never going to go back to the way of life that you had before. If I'm trying to replicate who I was before, that's guaranteed failure. Because that person doesn't exist anymore either . . . '**

I was deeply touched by the truth of this. Life is a moment-to-moment unfolding experience. Each moment is brand new, so we can never return to how life was before. Because there is no 'before'. There is only a life-long succession of nows.

This brings us to the final myth . . . .

Myth 4: Time is a healer

How often do you hear people say that 'time heals all wounds'? I know I have uttered these words many times in the past to comfort people who are in pain.

But is this true?

How do some people keep functioning as they were before their loss, when others struggle to find any peace or joy for months or even years?

Grieving can feel like an endlessly dark road with no light in sight. It can also arrive in random waves of intense emotion that engulf us, then quickly dissolve.

Khalil and his family tried different therapy and support groups for people who had been through similar kinds of bereavement. He said: 'I met one woman who had been going to the self-help group for 10 years. And I thought, this woman has been swallowed up by her grief. I realised the only person that was going to find a way to rebuild their mental strength was me.'

We tell each other that time is the healer. But it's not about time. The healer is beyond time or any other human construct.

Our natural capacity to experience new thought . . . to appreciate and perceive the world with new eyes . . . to have a sudden change of heart . . . what if this is the true healer? That quiet ever-present ordinary magic that brings renewed hope . . . that nudges you forward, gets you out of bed, energising you to continue and do more than just exist.

When I asked Khalil what helped him begin to heal and embrace life again, he described how random questions would pop into his mind like *'What would a doctor say to me'? What would my father, a psychiatrist say to me?'*

Then he would reflect and begin to act on some of the answers that came to him. It is such a beautiful example of the wisdom within.

He said: 'Resilience is there, it's built in, we use it daily. We don't regard it as a superpower or strength, because it's in motion all the time in lots of tiny, tiny, little ways.'

Khalil witnessed this innate resilience in his children, as he watched them adapting to a new normal . . . noticing them smile and laugh again, able to find joy in the physical absence of their brother Charlie.

I used to think the death of a loved one meant the end of those relationships. But I have learned that love and connection live on. Relationships never die because they are in our heart and soul.

Khalil and Nick described the unexpected 'gifts' they received. Nick found himself following a spiritual path, that brings insight into the illusions of ego and 'self'. He found a space within that took him by surprise. In a deeply moving moment, he said, 'I've taken this path because I think my son lives there.'

Khalil gained a new appreciation for what matters. 'I swear to God, I feel liberated. If I had a superpower . . . I think I would give everybody the ability to smell the roses every day. And that's why I call it

Charlie's gift. I'm living an emotionally more peaceful life. Peace. That's all I'm after now.'

Justin, who lost his wife to cancer soon after the birth of their first child, explained it like this:

> **'Your capacity for resilience proves itself in your ability to move on from a traumatic event and not be bound by it . . . not to be directed by it in the present and not to have future events be dominated by it.**
>
> **'[. . . .] it means that when this big ball swings into your life, in the shape of a traumatic event, [. . .] you know not to attach it to yourself . . . and it might knock a few things down. But you know not to stand in its way and let it take you with it. You understand its gravity . . . understand the scale and the knock-on effects, but you know that it moves through . . . '**

While I've been writing this book, my beautiful Mum passed away after a short and unexpected illness. Both my sister and I were by her side until her last breath. It was the most heart-breaking and intimate experience of my life. I miss her more than words can say but I know that her essence, her spirit and our deep love and connection is always here, because who we are is the divine energy of life itself and that never dies.

In essence

- -

♥ There is no right or wrong way to grieve . . . there is only what makes sense, given how *Mind, Thought* and *Consciousness* are manifesting in any moment.

♥ Peace is not the opposite of sadness. You can feel sad *and* be at peace.

♥ It's not about getting beyond grief. It's not about closure. It's about finding peace within our grieving.

♥ Life and death, loss and change are whatever we make them mean.

Bonus chapter materials here: http://www.chantalburns .com/bulletproof-chapter-8-grief-loss

chapter 9

You've got this!

'I am not afraid of storms,
for I am learning how to sail my ship.'

Louisa May Alcott (1832–1888)

You could find a thousand reasons why you can't or shouldn't do something. You need to wait until the time is right. You need to wait for the right feeling. You need to wait until you're smart enough. You need to wait for permission or approval. You need certainty. Before you know it, the moment has passed, and you realise you've been a passenger on the train of your life with fear in the driving seat.

When it comes to mental interference, none is more deceptive and destructive than insecurity. I'm talking about that feeling that renders you useless even though you know you're not.

Emotional insecurity ruins relationships with jealousy and resentment. It's behind our insatiable urge to consume what we don't need. Insecurity hijacks our common sense and drowns our intuition. It's the reason we passionately deny painful truths. We look away, distracting ourselves because it feels too hard to think about.

Insecurity makes you self-conscious. It steals your voice and stops you speaking up. Or it can do the very opposite and make you say and do things you later regret.

Our fears, unless seen for what they are, can rob the world of the beauty, power and brilliance that you are born with. Maybe you shrink back, deny your dreams, or play small.

Claudette was producing a podcast documentary 'My Dad Mr Brixton' about her trailblazing father.[1] As she began to make progress, her mind succumbed to stubborn whispers of self-doubt. The voice in her head told her she wasn't ready . . . it wasn't good enough . . . *she* wasn't good enough. Overwhelmed with worry, she began second guessing everything and, eventually, feeling overwhelmed, she pulled away, unsure of her project's fate. An essential piece of history was almost left in the past. But the calling to complete this labour of love was way bigger than her personal fears and she found herself back in the saddle.

As Shakespeare wrote, 'Our doubts are traitors, and make us lose the good we oft might win, by fearing to attempt.'[2]

Has insecurity ever stopped you from expressing yourself or taking action?

There are times when I've worried about what other people will think or how things will turn out. I've made excuses for holding back, convincing myself that those reasons were valid.

We think the past can determine the future. But the past can only exist now, as an expression of *Thought* in the moment.

That's why yesterday's insights won't necessarily solve tomorrow's problems.

History provides powerful lessons, but it doesn't dictate how we move forwards, unless we decide it does.

We think we need to control the future to feel secure and resilient now. But the future can only be influenced, never controlled. And a future moment can only exist in the stories we tell ourselves now.

Yet we pin our contentment, security and peace of mind on the past or on some goal, some event or someone 'out there' in an imagined future.

We outsource our well-being.

We postpone happiness.

We delay action.

When [. . . happens], then I will feel OK/ready/complete/good enough.

If [. . . doesn't happen] then I won't feel OK/ready/complete/good enough.

Elaine was having a crisis of confidence. 'If I don't get positive feedback, I question my work and my worth. But when people praise my work, I don't believe them. I'll find reasons why it's not valid or justified.' She knew it didn't make sense but wasn't sure how to move past it.

John is a serial entrepreneur. 'When the finances aren't good, I get anxious. And when things are going well, I worry. I feel insecure either way.'

If money could make us feel a certain way, then materially wealthy people would always be happier or feel more secure than those with far less material wealth. But that's not what happens, because we each have a different relationship with money, given how we are perceiving it.

We are born with the creativity to think up anything. We are born with the power to feel and experience the products of *Mind*, not the material world.

The illusion that emotional security can exist outside of *Consciousness* and outside of this present moment keeps us locked in a delusion, divorcing us from reality.

Yes but . . . if someone is continually told throughout their childhood that they are worthless or rubbish, then surely they will believe it and lack confidence as a result. Or if someone is given praise by their boss, they will feel more confident. Surely what others do or say must have an impact on how secure we do or don't feel?

Vanessa Feltz asked a similar question when she interviewed me on BBC Radio[3] after my first book came out. I could relate to this because I lived much of my life with what felt like a constant hum of insecurity, never feeling settled in myself.

When I was younger, my mum noticed how self-conscious I was, particularly with boyfriends. She would say, 'You need to relax and be yourself.' She always seemed so at ease with people. I didn't know how to be like that. I was so used to hiding my insecurities behind humour or hard work. I thought feeling insecure was part of my (permanent) makeup.

Turns out that we're not born feeling insecure or anxious, but conditioning is a powerful process. We learn to think and behave in ways that become habits. Those habits and patterns are part of how we survive and adapt. Whether it's stopping at traffic lights or protecting ourselves. It's the same system at play.

As a young child, John learned how to disappear from his drunken dad to protect himself. While it was a life saver at seven, he (unknowingly) carried this safety strategy into his adult life. Whenever he felt uneasy, he would detach or hide away from the world, and this would distance him from the people and situations that he wanted to feel closer to. Now looking back, he can honour and appreciate the innate wisdom that helped to keep him safe as a child. He also knows he can leave that safety strategy in the past like an old pair of shoes . . . well-worn but no longer fitting.

Insecurity is a temporary state of mind, not a pathological condition.

It doesn't need to be fixed or medicated. The antidote to insecure feelings is to recognise what they are.

> **Yes but . . .** what about food insecurity or financial insecurity . . . that's not mind-made is it?

Having sufficient food, water, shelter and care is essential for any species to survive and live well. But the most common insecurity, at least in the developed world, is when our sense of 'self' or ego feels threatened.

Useful distinction:
situational security vs spiritual/ psychological security

In one of our local community groups, we work with residents and local leaders on issues including food, water and energy security.[4] These are all examples of situational security. But our natural capacity to act from clarity and compassion is what makes the biggest difference to how we adapt, solve problems and meet the challenges and disruptions coming our way.

Emotional insecurity gets instantly created in the moment that we mentally split the Principle of Thought from the feelings, emotions and sensations it produces.

When you attach feelings of (in)security to situations, people, places or objects, this creates an unhealthy attachment or avoidance. It makes you behave in ways you otherwise wouldn't.

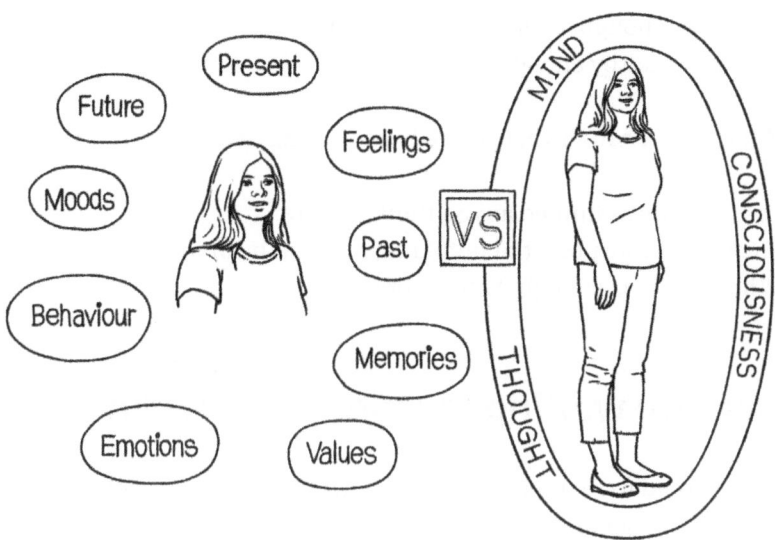

We have all these different 'things' separated from each other and from our own mind. But it's the mind that separates them in the first place.

Our inner spiritual life and outer physical/material life are one.

Do you think you need to be a certain type of person to fulfil your ambitions?

If only I was more . . . *then* . . .
   I can't do . . . because I'm not . . . enough

The stories, rules and reasons we give ourselves are the energy of *Mind* masquerading as facts.

We justify our actions and behaviour on a fabricated self-image.

We hold back and stop ourselves because we think we're not enough . . .

not smart enough, confident enough, articulate enough, attractive enough, wealthy enough . . .

What's the 'enough' that you've been waiting to be?

You are only as limited as you think you are.
You are infinite potential unfolding moment by moment.
Who you are is enough. You've got this!

Are you waiting for the 'right' feeling?

If I'd waited to feel secure enough, I would never have left the (perceived) security of a job to start a business back in 1999. If I had waited to feel like a good enough writer, I wouldn't have written my first book or considered a second one. If I had waited until I felt ready, I wouldn't have set up a leadership school or a community choir. I could have given myself endless excuses not to go ahead.

Do you think you need to feel a particular way before you take that leap, speak your mind, or try something new? Are you waiting for the perfect conditions or the perfect time?

If Hannah had waited to feel a certain way, she wouldn't have created award-winning vegan brand OGGS™. She and her business partner had zero experience in food production and retail. 99% of what they were doing was new to them.

> **'I'd never even stepped into a food factory. We launched 700 supermarkets with seven skews in two weeks, which I think is pretty unheard of and it was very much the capacity to not worry about my worrying or think about my thinking and allow that to pass through.'**

Her decision to act wasn't contingent on how confident or knowledgeable she felt. Instead, she listened to her heart and followed her instincts. Hannah was moved by a sense of purpose, inspired by her desire to remove animal product from the food chain. She knew they had a lack of experience in this area, but she also knew they had the ability to learn and adapt as they went.

Before creating OGGS™, Hannah had been learning about the inside>out psychology through our Conscious Leadership programme. 'The biggest thing that I learned is that my thinking isn't who I am, and my thinking isn't what I am.'

> **'In not getting too caught up in what's going on in my head, it flows away more quickly, and I get back to doing the job versus worrying about whether I can do the job.'**

Hannah also realised that an essential element of leading well is freeing people up by showing them how to remove unnecessary mental noise, so their creativity can flow more easily.

Are you waiting for things to be a particular way?

Hannah became aware of the structure, standards, rules and requirements that she'd constructed for how her life should be and, when the reality didn't reflect her expectations, she would get stressed. But, when it matched, she felt more relaxed.

'And that just meant that I spent a lot of time trying to put lots of things in boxes to make it look like I thought it needed to look,' Hannah explained to me.

It's not just our own ideas that can keep us stuck. We also try to live up to other people's expectations. We think that, if we satisfy their hopes of us, we will make them happy or proud. We're afraid to let them down.

Giles was brought up being told how smart and capable he was. His parents made their plans for him clear early on. When he was diagnosed with multiple sclerosis and lost his eyesight at 24, the life that others had charted for him was no longer feasible.

> **'The illness absolved me from all of that because I didn't have to have a conventionally successful graduate career anymore. I could find the things that I loved to do . . . wanted to do. And luckily for me, I did. So just following the joy became part of it.'**

Giles felt liberated from his family's expectations and felt free to forge his own path. But he'd always been free to choose. He just hadn't realised that.

Expectations are *Thought*.

We all have ideas about how things *should* be and how things *should* turn out. We believe these rules and imaginary outcomes are responsible for how we feel now.

We make up preferences about what we like and dislike. When we get attached to these preferences as if they are facts, we can spend our lives in a perpetual state of discontent and unhappiness because our likes and dislikes can limit our experience of life and what we think is possible. We innocently set ourselves up for disappointment. Even our hopes can mislead us if they're not grounded in reality.

The myth of the comfort zone

Suzy joined the choir to learn to sing, boost her confidence and make new friends. After two sessions, she left saying, 'It's too far outside my comfort zone.'

Have you ever stopped yourself doing something that you were inspired to do for the same reason?

Thought experiment

- -

In the context of 'comfort zones', reflect on the questions below and notice what comes to mind. There are no right or wrong answers.

What is comfort? What does comfort mean to you?

. . . .

If you think about going outside of your comfort zone, what are you going *outside of*?

. . . .

And what's beyond the 'comfort zone'?

. . . .

- -

Comfort is in the mind of the beholder . . . it's a label, a projection, a feeling.

Suzy left the choir because of a 'zone' that exists within her imagination, but that felt very real. She left because she couldn't be with the discomfort of some passing thoughts and feelings.

When you recognise concepts like 'comfort zones' for what they are – *made up* – you are instantly free from the constraints of these mental constructs.

There's nothing beyond your comfort zone, except what you think. Because *Thought* creates the zone in the first place.

If you judge what you can or can't do by how confident or insecure you feel in the moment, it means you have forgotten that your true nature is boundless and free.

Joan Rivers was an American comedian. Her first big break didn't happen until she was in her forties when she became one of the hottest acts on the comedy circuit. And, despite feeling insecure, she went on stage night after night, and had audiences howling in their seats. Joan was a true pioneer, who spoke honestly about her own insecurities, and didn't pander to popularity. She paved the way for many of the greatest female comedian of our time.

> **'Security is mostly a superstition. It does not exist in nature, nor do the children of [women] as a whole experience it. Avoiding danger is no safer in the long run than outright exposure. Life is either a daring adventure or nothing.'**
>
> **Helen Keller, activist, author and educator**

We don't know our limits because many of us rarely go beyond what scares us. Our minds get seduced into staying in the illusion of safety.

You don't have to be confident to begin. But you must begin if you want to get more confident.

Are you attaching your emotional security or peace of mind to some future scenario?

'What are you looking for?'
'My glasses'
'They're on your face!'

We spend our lives looking for something that's already onboard.

Feeling scared has no bearing on what you are capable of.

One is not connected to the other, except in your mind.

What are you waiting for? You've got this!

The only thing you can be certain of

In my early twenties, I would regularly visit Mags, a local tarot card reader.

'Will things turn out OK?' 'Will this relationship last?' 'Am I making the right decision?' I was looking for answers. Perhaps she was channelling some divine source (she always seemed so perceptive) or maybe she was just good at reassuring me, but she always delivered.

When we don't know what's going to happen in the future, it can feel threatening. We struggle with the lack of control. We make up stories to make sense of things, so we can feel more secure and settled. Mags could have told me anything, so desperate was my need for certainty.

Fear of the unknown has inspired a multi-million pound industry dedicated to relieving us of our worries, fears and doubts.

The 'estimated arrival time' screens on train platforms are designed to help passengers alleviate their uncertainty anxiety. It's OK, we tell ourselves, because we know how long we have to wait. But the only difference between knowing and not knowing, is what our mind does with that information (or lack of).

Planning for the future requires being in the present

Studies have shown that worrying about job loss takes a bigger toll on our health and well-being than losing a job. Similarly, research participants who were told that they had a 50% chance of receiving an electric shock felt far more anxious than participants who believed they were going to receive the shock.

Imagination, anticipation and expectation play a major role in our anxieties and discontent. Fantasising, worrying, catastrophising, future proofing, scenario planning. . . .

We spend so much mental energy thinking about the future. Nothing wrong with that. Planning and creating is an essential part of living in this physical world.

The problem is that so much of our mental energy is used trying to control or manage an imagined future that has no power over your resilience and capability in the moment.

> **'Uncertainty is the only certainty there is and learning to live with insecurity is the only security.'**
> **John Allen Paulos, Professor of Mathematics**

After Giles was diagnosed with multiple sclerosis, he went to the Science Museum to learn more. 'I looked at a book [. . .] in which the doctor starts by saying, "Everyone says I shouldn't write this because it would be very depressing for people who've been diagnosed."'

Giles goes on to say, 'There's this acutely painful, acutely disabling, chronic condition with no known cause and no known cure [. . .] your own immune system attacks your brain and spinal cord, leaving scars . . . and it can paralyse you. I honestly thought that this was all imminent. I was 24. Just about to turn 25.'

The more he read, and the more he listened to the 'experts', the worse he felt. The future they painted was full of uncontrollable pain and suffering. He felt like he had an axe poised above his head.

One day, his girlfriend Sooz said, 'Let's not call it multiple sclerosis, because they don't know what that is. And we don't know what that is. So don't coach yourself to follow a predetermined path. Let's just say MS stands for Mysterious Symptoms.'

She could hear how Giles was thinking himself into a future that didn't exist.

They were dealing with a condition the medical field had limited knowledge of but Giles had become certain of his fate and fallen into the Knowledge trap.

'Sooz kept saying this thing to me – she kept saying, "Soften the will."'

'I was young, I was intelligent and brittle. I had positions. I had prejudices, as in, I was disposed towards certain opinions. And I had to have an answer to all sorts of questions. I had to have an opinion ready for any situation.

'And so I'd read all this stuff about Multiple Sclerosis and said, OK, that's what this means. And eventually, I was able to embrace the point of . . . I don't fucking know anything. I really don't know anything . . .

'I did realise that if I was going to spend my life being afraid of what I couldn't see, I was never going to leave my bed. I didn't want that. So it becomes a choice.'

Uncertainty is the experience of not knowing. The unknown is neither good nor bad. It has no inherent qualities because it doesn't exist. And when it comes into existence through human consciousness, it will mean whatever you think it does.

'The unknown can be a very joyful and a very welcoming space. It's a creative space. So for example, when I'm telling stories, I don't know what I'm going to say next. I don't know how I'm going to tell it. I create a story as I tell it,' Giles told me.

What a great metaphor for life. We're each creating our own story breath by breath, thought by thought, moment to moment.

What we think is possible (or not possible), determines what we entertain and what we ignore or discount. And this in turn shapes all subsequent feelings, emotions and perceptions. So it's helpful to become more conscious of what you believe and challenge your assumptions. 'Is this *really* true?' has become one of my favourite questions.

I've realised that arguing or denying something prior to investigating is the epitome of ignorance and I've been ignorant many times!

We cling onto what we think we know, because we believe it makes us feel secure. For example,

'If I know (what is going to happen/all the facts/that I'm right), then . . . I can plan better/feel better/do better.'

There is immense power in recognising how much we do not and cannot know. Just consider the vastness of the universe and the mysteries it holds. Even the most knowledgeable scientists realise there is so much they don't yet understand.

What if, in our daily lives, we could approach situations with that same humility or wonder? What if you were less certain about what you think you know for sure?

Imagine how this sense of wonder and curiosity could deepen connections and open new doors for understanding and growth in your life.

> **'Our perceptions are a kind of story that we create to make sense of the world. And just like any other story, they can be changed, rewritten, or discarded altogether.'**
>
> **Prof. Donald Hoffman**

Living well with uncertainty isn't about control or wishful thinking. It's about finding peace and perspective in the midst of ambiguity. It's when we recognise we are plugged into the intelligence of the universe and can allow ourselves to be guided.

If history has taught us anything, it's that we can thrive in the unknown and adapt fast.

Life is improvisation. We are all winging it because we cannot know what we will think and feel in the next moment. Every moment is brand new.

You are designed to live in a world of uncertainty and flux because flux is the nature of life. We are designed to imagine, wonder, create and discover.

Apart from the certainty that we are thinkers, there is no ultimate guarantee about anything. All we have are predictions, models and assumptions. These can be helpful. For example, we're in an ecological emergency, so we need to learn, adapt and innovate, all of which are natural qualities.

We are born with the power of insight...to have a new thought, a change of heart and see the world with new eyes in any moment. In this way we are spiritually and psychologically resilient by design.

Whatever the next moment brings, *you've got this!*

Do you know when to quit?

I've stayed in relationships even though every fibre in my body was telling me to leave. Fear of being alone, starting again, hurting others are some of the reasons I gave myself for sticking with situations that weren't healthy or right.

Have you ever kept going when you should have quit?

Mary had been working 50–60 hours a week, for months. She was exhausted and on the brink of burnout. There was little support from senior management. Everyone around her was fraying at the edges. Social workers and team leaders were being signed off sick while the volume and complexity of cases was increasing.

'I'm not resilient enough. I should be able to cope with this. I'm a failure. I'm going to let everyone down' were some of the thoughts that kept her awake at night. And then she saw how her thinking was trapping her. 'I was making up a story. None of it was true. When I realised this, it was liberating. I felt empowered to do the right thing.'

Mary knew she could no longer carry the risk being put on her by a failing system. She'd been telling her senior managers for months that it was dangerous for the children, families and her team of social workers, but nothing had changed.

Despite feeling exhausted and overwhelmed, Mary had absolute clarity about what needed to be done. She went to the head of service and told them everything that was going on. And, when she was done, with a heavy heart, she quit.

She told me:

> **'If I didn't understand the principles, I would have self-loathing, telling myself I am shit. I would have felt guilty, but I don't. This was what I had to do.**
>
> **'I'm not broken. The system is broken. We have been failed by the organisation. We've got managers holding back and not being honest about all the problems because they are concerned it will reflect badly on them. This is the danger when self-image comes before safety. But I can get my big hairy bollocks out. I can be a voice for people who don't have a voice.'**

We can silence ourselves with fear, but we can also do what needs to be done and say what needs to be said, even when we feel afraid.

> **Resilience is not just about staying power. It's also about the power of leaving.**

What are you waiting for? *You've got this!*

Don't worry, it'll probably never happen!

Laura is 14 years old. She often feels self-conscious and insecure. She constantly worries about what other people think of her to the point of paranoia. If she notices someone looking at her, she instantly assumes they must judging her in some way, which only makes her want to retreat and hide away from the world.

'I tell her they're probably not even talking about her. I tell her she doesn't have to worry about stuff that will probably never happen,' her mum told me.

How many times have you heard or thought that?

Like any loving parent, Rachel wanted to help her daughter relax and feel better. She couldn't bear to see Laura struggling and feeling so scared and lost.

And she's right. Much of what we worry about will never happen. It's also true that much of what we don't think about *will* happen. Giles could never have anticipated what would come his way. Neither could Khalil or Chris or Hannah.

But this isn't a 'don't worry it might never happen' book.

What if the worst thing you could imagine *did* happen?

Would you still be resilient at your core? Would well-being, courage, clarity and compassion still be within? Would all feelings and sensations still be coming from the energy behind life?

The answer is always *yes* because you're always experiencing reality from the inside>out. Like Gravity, the Inside>out principles never take a day off. They don't cease to exist just because you have doubts.

True resilience is knowing that, whatever situations arise, they cannot dictate how you feel or behave in the moment. You can handle whatever life throws at you because you always have what you need inside.

Living a guided life

What would life be like if you knew there was a pre-existing spiritual intelligence . . . a source of wisdom that is always trying to express itself through you?

What if you didn't have to try and control everything and instead could just tap into that deeper wisdom?

> **'Insight is the quiet whisper of wisdom that arises from the depths of our being.'**
>
> **Deepak Chopra, author and clinical director**

I managed to get myself out of bed that morning. I found myself in the kitchen smoking. It was 7 am. I wasn't a smoker. I made myself a coffee when I usually drink tea. I looked out of the window, but I couldn't see anything except the mess in my head. I remember opening the cupboard door and having this panicky thought, 'How am I going to pay my mortgage next month, how will I pay my bills?'

I'd stopped working. I stopped everything I was doing. I was heart-broken and felt empty and I could just about get out of bed. That was the biggest step I could take and that was only because my friend would call every morning to make sure I was up and breathing. As I stood there, my phone rang. It was my best friend: 'How are you?' I said, 'I think I need to see the doctor. I need some help.' 'What do you mean?' she asked. 'I need some pills or something. I'm depressed.'

And then she said something that could have seemed blasé but it wasn't.

'There's nothing wrong with you. You're just very, very sad. But you're OK. You're going to be OK.' And this wasn't a superficial attempt to make me feel better.

What I heard was, 'It's OK to feel sad.' I heard that I am not broken. The truth of this sneaked past my stories, sadness and hurt. I got off the phone, smoked another cigarette and drank another coffee. And I still wondered, how am I going to pay my bills? But within a couple of days something had shifted. I started to reach out to people. I made phone calls and began to create possibilities again. I was still sad and the tears came every day, but I was working. Slowly but surely healing happened.

The power of insight – to realise, learn, discover and experience new realities in every moment is your birth right.

After his son passed away, insight and love got Khalil out of bed. It kept bringing him reasons to continue to slowly find joy again.

Suzy realised her insecure thinking is not who she is at her core.

In the moment that she saw this, a life-long belief that she was unable to be herself and was destined to feel uncomfortable around others collapsed.

Archie realised that, although he was physically imprisoned, his mind was free.

There is sight and then there is really seeing. Giles discovered his true passion for storytelling and lives a life full of love and gratitude. His real vision has no boundaries.

Every positive change in our world begins with a moment of insight, a collapsing of ego, a change of heart.

Insight arrives in unexpected moments. It takes us by surprise. Sometimes it takes your breath away with its power and precision. It's always tailor-made for you. That's why someone else's realisations and wisdom, while helpful or interesting, don't necessarily provide you with the answers you are looking for.

Insight is the spark of light in the dark. It puts a question to rest. It's the gift that keeps on giving. Whenever you feel lost or confused, wisdom will deliver, and you will find your footing again.

You are designed to thrive. *You've got this!*

Insecurity is *Thought* not things

It might seem like there are lots of things that can make you feel insecure, but when you remember these are all manifestations of one cause, it simplifies your life.

'We have to see in the singular if we want to find truth.'

Syd Banks

Much of our insecurity stems from fear of feelings.

But remember that you were born to feel.

Feelings are feedback on your mind's activity in the moment.

They don't need to be fixed. They only need to be acknowledged and understood.

Emotions are energy. They can't harm you.

There is no emotion, however strong or intense, that has any special power over you. You're always psychologically and spiritually secure, no matter how you feel in any moment.

'I learned that courage was not the absence of fear, but the triumph over it. The brave man is not he who does not feel afraid, but he who conquers that fear.'

Nelson Mandela

By continually stripping away myth and misunderstanding, we discover that resilience is the same for everyone. It's not a personal accomplishment. It's not time- or event-based. It has no conditions attached to it. If you're alive, resilience is your nature.

And this is what it means to be bulletproof. It's not about being detached from your emotions. It's not about being tough. It doesn't mean that you'll never feel insecure or scared or that you should stay in a situation that doesn't feel right. Being bulletproof is knowing you are free and safe to lean deeply and fully into any emotion. It means you have what you need to safely surf the biggest waves.

To love, to ache in times of loss, to want justice, to want to hug that person we see suffering . . . all of this is part of our humanity and our connection to something greater than any one of us.

Maybe you feel scared to take a chance, tell the truth, write that book, ask that person out, challenge the status quo, leave that abusive relationship, ask for help or speak out when others are trying to silence you. But remember that your fears are not telling you anything about how resilient you are. They are not telling you anything about your true nature.

Your spirit is unbreakable.

You are bulletproof. You've got this.

The journey continues

'Insight is the ultimate rebellion of the mind against its limitations.'

Ralph Waldo Emerson

What's next?

You might be wondering how you can continue this journey or how you can share this with others, whether it's in your personal or work life.

Below are some useful resources to tap into which include podcasts, videos, courses, articles, research and more. If you don't find what you're looking for, please get in touch!

Stay in the conversation

If you just want to stay connected and get free resources including podcasts, articles, videos etc., then subscribe here:

http://www.chantalburns.com/bulletproof-freebies

'What about *This*?'

If there are topics or issues that are important to you that don't seem to have been addressed in the book, then visit this page

http://www.chantalburns.com/bulletproof-whataboutthis

For coaches, counsellors and facilitators

If you want to help others and you would welcome some guidance for how to increase the impact of your coaching or counselling practice, including a powerful coaching framework, visit this link:

https://www.consciousleadershipschool.com/bulletproof-coaching-counselling/

For business/work life

The Conscious Leadership School provides programmes, individual and group coaching and other educational services to leaders and teams within organisations. If you want to remove the unnecessary mental noise and interference that gets in the way of doing great work, get in touch here:

www.consciousleadershipschool.com

For social justice and climate resilience

If you are a climate resilience or social justice champion and you want to find like-minded people and groups to connect with, visit the link below or scan the QR code for some great resources and groups you can get involved with.

http://consciousleadershipschool.com/social-justice-climate-resilience/

For recommended resources

For a constantly updated list of recommended books, podcasts and other great materials, scan the QR code or visit the following link:

http://www.chantalburns.com/bulletproof-recommended-books-and-resources/

Voices from the field: A collection of conversations with practitioners

To read and listen to more of these, please visit:
http://www.chantalburns.com/bulletproof-voices-from-the-field
or scan the QR code below:

Dr Rani Bora is a holistic psychiatrist and mental wealth coach whose specialist interest is safe deprescribing of psychiatric medication and helping people explore who they are beyond their diagnosis or mental suffering.

Chantal: How did you come to learn about the inside>out psychology?

Rani: Like many people, I've been a seeker and my justification was that if I learn something that's useful for me, then I can take it to my patients. That was my motivation. It started with life coaching, doing one thing after another and always thinking, 'Is there something else?' But it felt like coaching, positive psychology, and similar, could not be applied to people with mental illness, because mental illness is at the other end of the spectrum and those kinds of techniques don't really work.

So, through my searching, I came across the 'Three Principles' understanding, and had a huge insight. I realised that, although I thought of myself as a recovery-oriented psychiatrist, always wanting to do good for my patients, in reality I was seeing them as broken and I wanted to fix them.

So that was the pivotal moment for me where things just shifted and after that I couldn't go back to how I used to work with people.

Chantal: Tell me more about how you viewed psychiatry and mental health before this insight and how it informed your approach?

Rani: I saw mental illness as, in a way, incurable. You know, you just live with it.

You get relief of the symptoms by taking medication, having CBT and learning coping strategies. And you do your best to live a meaningful life, but that was it. That was my worldview . . . that these are long-standing cases of depression, psychosis, bipolar, you name it, and my view was OK, we can only do so much. And people will have to be on medication for a long, long time.

Then when I came across the Inside>out principles, I began to listen to what was not working in psychiatry. I didn't realise back then that these medications we were giving people were actually, in the long run, doing more harm than good. So going back to your question, I always felt like the best we could do is give them well-being tools. It was a lot of 'do this', 'do that', we'll give you medicine, we'll give you CBT . . . and you have to do all these activities or you can do mindfulness. These were more like quick fixes. But not deep, let me put it that way.

And now, in the short time I have with patients in my NHS clinic, it's enough to share a little bit about the principles and then point them to all the amazing resources out there. Especially I point them to Sydney Banks if they are open.

I cannot imagine not having come across this because what I see now is unbelievable. It's just unbelievable. And so I'm very grateful. This is now part of what I do and how I show up.

Chantal: When you say it's unbelievable, can you talk a little about this? How does this inform the way that you now work with people? Share some of the impact that you're seeing and how it's different to before.

Rani: Yes, I think the main thing is . . . all these labels we put on people, you know, they are just labels. And I love to quote Bill Pettit that 'diagnosis is not who you are, but where you are'. It's just what I see in my patients and it's about going beyond the diagnosis. And what I know now is that if we just look at the symptoms, we're always firefighting . . . we're always trying to reduce and dampen the symptoms. It's like with the medications . . . we are just numbing the experiences, instead of helping people to see beyond that, to where the experience is coming from.

And to illustrate the point, most of the people who come to secondary care, like mental health services, once they have been in the system for some time, once they have a diagnosis, invariably, over time, I have seen them end up with multiple diagnoses and on multiple medications. And despite all the evidence-based treatment we give them, which is mainly medication and psychological therapy, most still seem to be chronically unwell, or they don't seem to get any better. And with one of my patients as an example, he's on many different drugs. But what's interesting is that as I'm helping him reduce his medications and at the same time helping him to connect with his innate well-being, he seems to be getting better.

If I were to just reduce the medication, I don't think it would be a success. I don't think they would benefit as much, or they could but the ill-health symptoms come back. But while I'm reducing the medications safely, and at the same time introducing them to the Inside>out principles, what I'm witnessing is that something else is available for people.

For example, a client who has been on all these medications for many years, to treat him for depression and anxiety. He's not only been reading Second Chance, but he's going through all Syd Banks' resources and one day he comes back and says 'a few weeks ago, if you had told me that I would be feeding wild birds, I would have laughed at your face, because I don't do that kind of stuff.' And now he's taking pleasure in feeding the birds.

That's a small step to recovery but I'm talking about someone who had lost complete hope. And now he is feeling very hopeful. And this is not a technique like 'do some bird feeding' . . . there's something else coming from within and he's beginning to feel that. And of course he's on a journey because he's on so many medications that I need to taper off. But that's an example of going beyond the diagnosis.

Then there's a person in my Beyond Diagnosis coaching programme who has psychosis. And he also hears voices. He is beginning to see the true nature of the voices and, at the same time, he's *really* connecting to the principles. We had a book reading on *Second Chance* and then we had another reading on *In Quest of the Pearl*. And I can see that something is landing for people. And they are also making sense of the psychosis, for example, being an illusion of the mind. Now my traditional training including CBT, would have never prepared me for the deeper connection and conversations I'm having with people and the profound shifts that I am witnessing.

Chantal: Dr Bill Pettit has said that as a psychiatrist and MD, he was trained in mental illness but never trained in mental health. It's clear to me that the direction that you are pointing patients, is very different when you're listening for their innate health, versus listening with a focus on illness. Because you're not seeing them as sick.

Rani: Yes, there's another psychiatrist, Pam Pappas. I saw a Facebook post which resonated deeply because she said that for a long time her practice was trauma informed. But since coming across the principles, her practice has also become wisdom informed and I thought 'that's amazing'. All these conferences you go to, they are talking about being trauma informed. I understand where they're coming from, but now my practice has evolved to being wisdom informed and I'm borrowing her word for it.

Yes there is trauma and misfortune, but all the stuff that happens to us cannot touch our innate health. Nothing from the past can really touch the deep space or core self or whatever you want to call it. And that was a major shift for me because in the past, I always felt sorry for people. I see my colleagues do the same. When they talk about patients, they feel sorry for them, worrying that they're doomed for life because of the trauma.

And now I love having these conversations with people if they're willing to because I can point them to the fact that yes the trauma happened. It was horrible. It shouldn't have happened. But it did and it hasn't broken them because the essence of them is untouchable, limitless, formless, however you want to describe it. So now anyone can sit in front of me and can talk about all kinds of trauma and I don't get fazed by it. I'm not thinking 'Oh this is hopeless'. Whereas before, I used to dread these kinds of conversations, because I didn't have anything else to offer other than sympathy, empathy, medication or signposting them for psychological therapies. Now, I have a more profound way of connecting to someone. And without feeling overwhelmed. You can really settle down and go deeper into a place of love.

So this is a massive change in my work. It's about looking inwards for the answer rather than looking out there, for example with medication or supplements. And some of these might be needed, but this is definitely an invitation to go within and, through self-enquiry, explore the gift we are always carrying with us even though we might not know that. And this really helps me with all the patients that I see . . . knowing that they have mental wealth within . . . that's the constant . . .

Chantal: I recently heard a high profile advocate of mental health say 'Depression is a disease that can't be cured and the best that you can do is learn to manage the symptoms,' What's your view? I ask this because it seems at odds with the growing body of work and evidence related to depression.

Rani: When someone has depression, there could be so many contributing factors. Someone holding on to that kind of belief (that it's a disease that can't be cured) is trapped in an antiquated model of thinking . . . that once you are given a label, nothing can shift but actually things *can* shift. But if people are still getting very lost, they could attract more diagnoses. So someone who has got, for example, chronic depression (which was unheard of in the past as depression is meant to be episodic), soon they could get chronic anxiety, they could get agoraphobia, they could get an eating disorder. So yes, if we are getting more and more lost in our thinking, and if someone is identifying with a label and they're saying 'This is who I am,' then the symptoms can become chronic.

More and more evidence is showing that depression is not straightforward. Yes it can be debilitating, but there are lots of different things contributing to it, for example, inflammation, lifestyle, etc. And if you make changes, it can be reversed. Even Type II diabetes can be reversed. But what I'm also saying is that not everyone is able to have that shift. They might be doing all the right things but if they're attached to the belief that 'This cannot change,' they are misusing the power of *Thought*, and they will be right because it's like a self-fulfilling prophecy.

I have seen many people recover and not because they have increased medication but because they had a powerful insight.

Chantal: What about the theory of chemical imbalance? This is often cited as the cause of depression. I've been researching this for some time, and it doesn't seem to stack up.

Rani: The latest evidence, and what more psychiatrists are admitting, is that this was just a theory. Depression is more complex, they now say. This myth has been busted because there is no evidence whatsoever that depression is caused by a chemical imbalance. Dr Joanna Moncrieff[1] and Mike Horowitz (for his work on antidepressants) need to get a Nobel Peace Prize for their work here.

Chantal: I am making some clear distinctions in my book about what resilience is and what it isn't. I can hear in what you are sharing that you also see resilience as an innate, pre-existing fact?

Rani: What most people are talking about is 'acquired' resilience. But I'm talking about innate resilience. And that's a subtle but crucial distinction because yes we need to eat good food and exercise, maybe take supplements but then we're talking about the form. What you're pointing to is clearly the formless . . . it's innate.

Chantal: So, as a psychiatrist, would you say that innate resilience is the true healer, and not 'acquired' resilience?

Rani: Yes. Like today at this conference I attended, people talked about diet, herbs and supplements and all this amazing stuff. I know so many people who take all these and they say life is still crap. They're still unwell. That's because these things are not the true healer. I really love what Bill Pettit talks about here . . . that there is only one cause of mental illness. It's chronic stress and of course you can understand what it does to the hypothalamic-pituitary-adrenal axis, with all the inflammation, the effect on our immune system, it's impact on physical and mental health and for which you're trying to give people medicine, supplements, etc.

And he says the root cause, or the only solution to eradicate mental illness, is peace of mind. So that's the true healer. And it's a precious treasure, a gift we have all been given. And the only barrier is ourselves . . . our own mind.

Dr Rita Shuford has been a practising counsellor, mentor, trainer and supervisor for 52 years, working in the field of mental health and healthcare. She has been a 'Three principles' practitioner for 46 years and a licensed psychologist for 38 years. Dr Shuford has taught in universities and led educational programmes and services in schools, community, businesses and hospitals.

Chantal: What brought you to the Inside>out principles?

Rita: Like most if not all health care providers, I felt a calling to help others. As a young person, my heart would go out to family and friends who were struggling with life challenges and I would do what I could to ease their burdens. Being somewhat reserved, I tended to listen and observe. My inclination was to look for the good and potential in people. When I found this challenging, I would get curious. I wondered, how can I create a connection that goes beyond the surface, to the core of their being? I was sure that if I could connect with them, heart to heart, soul to soul, I could bypass the barriers of fear and insecurity and get to know their real essence. I had plenty of insecurities myself, so I figured we were in the same boat. I could really empathise.

I love learning about how people tick from a spiritual/philosophical and psychological perspective. I was most drawn to human potential theorists and practitioners like Maslow, Allport, Adler, Dreikurs, Virginia Satir, Carl Rogers, C.S. Lewis, Einstein, William James, to name a few. I pursued and completed a Masters Degree in Counselling Psychology in 1971. I continued to study many theories and techniques in psychology and counselling. I figured that if something held true value it would enhance my own well-being and would also help others be happier and more secure in their own lives.

Back then there were over 450 approaches in the field of counselling/therapy, often conflicting. When I applied some of these approaches to myself and my work with clients, the initial hope of lasting change seemed to fade time and time again. Given that all these theories, practices and techniques were about the human being, I felt convinced there was something we were overlooking. I grew increasingly certain there was a missing link in our current understanding of how people tick and what it takes to be mentally healthy and happy.

In 1976, I took a sabbatical from my job with two goals in mind: 1) decide whether to pursue a doctorate in psychology and 2) find the missing link in our understanding of the human psyche. At the start of this search, I had lunch with a respected colleague and friend, Dr Roger Mills, director of the Lane County Community Mental Health Center. We had worked together, collaborating on community projects and grants.

At lunch he told me about a recent encounter with a man named Sydney Banks whose ideas and teachings offered the promise and potential to reduce and possibly alleviate human suffering. Dr Mills was intrigued and hopeful. He told me there were tapes of talks by Mr Banks at the University bookstore for students in his Community Mental Health classes. He was planning a visit to Salt Spring Island, where Sydney Banks lived, with hopes of delving deeper and learning more from him. I listened and wished him well as he did for me in my search.

Over the next eight to nine months, I spent a lot of time reflecting and exploring university courses. I had just gone through an amicable divorce and was beginning a new relationship but had a lot of questions about what it takes to be genuinely happy. And I couldn't shake this feeling that I was getting close to finding the missing link. I knew I would recognise it when I found it.

I finally entered the PhD program in Counselling Psychology. Then two weeks later, out of the blue, I remembered the tapes Dr Mills had mentioned. I hadn't seen him for close to a year. I went to the bookstore to check if there were any tapes left from his classes. There were just two and, to my surprise, one was called 'The Missing Link'. Curious to hear what Mr Banks had to say, I sat down in my apartment with my boyfriend and listened. About five minutes into the tape, the penny dropped. In that moment, I knew without a doubt that I'd found what I had been searching for all this time . . . the answer to alleviating human suffering, regardless of past or present conditions or circumstances. At first, I couldn't articulate what I was hearing but I knew he was saying that healthy psychological functioning is a moment to moment possibility for every human being, no exceptions. Just the appearance of exceptions.

Chantal: Can you share some of your early insights and the implications in your life?

Rita: What I experienced and saw deeply was that reality and human experience is being created from within moment to moment. The ideas being taught and perpetuated in traditional psychology were based on an innocent misunderstanding of how our minds work and what determines how we feel, react and behave. This meant that every client I saw had the potential to live with and from an unconditional sense of well-being and peace, able to thrive personally and professionally. Resilience got redefined as innate – meaning that it's naturally built into every human being, irrespective of age, life experiences, events, conditions, diagnosis, etc.

I began to understand that the missing link was spiritual, not religious, and defined as universal principles of *Mind*, *Consciousness* and *Thought*. And these principles simplify life . . . they provide a unifying deeper order and understanding for the field of psychology and psychiatry.

Chantal: What does this mean in practice?

Rita: I have worked with people from all walks of life and diagnostic categories. Without exception I know that innate wisdom/

mental health is at our core. This means the well-being we seek is innocently covered up by the way we are perceiving and using the creative power of *Thought* in the moment. I've never lost hope that at any moment a client can wake up, break free of their belief that something outside their own mind has the power to determine their experience 'now'. Guiding clients to their own common sense and wisdom, is an organic process that happens in the moment.

Chantal: What are some of the most significant changes you've experienced because of this understanding and awareness?

Rita: My personal experience of life became more joyful. To be happy and at peace for no reason became a reality of my life. My relationship with my boyfriend deepened, leading us to marry. Over the 40+ years we were together our relationship kept getting better and better. We were able to understand and navigate our differences with more grace, knowing we were living in separate realities, created from within. Disagreements stopped escalating into full-blown arguments about who is right and who is wrong. We began to trust that if we took a step back, our minds would naturally calm down and we would get a shift in perspective that comes with the wisdom and thinking you need to move forward in a healthy, harmonious way.

This has been the basis of my life and work for over 40 years.

I've seen amazing transformations out of the blue and I've watched people find increasing levels of well-being in themselves and in their lives. I've also seen folks who were stuck in their suffering, caught in the illusion of innocent beliefs and not yet ready to hear. Yet I remained and do remain hopeful that they will wake up to their true nature and regain their innate ability to enjoy life and work, living with inner peace and well-being, no matter what.

Dr Cheryl Bond has worked in the corporate learning and development field for 40 years. She has been helping leaders and teams increase their effectiveness and personal well-being for over 20 years. Most of her clients are engineers, scientists and researchers who appreciate the logic of a principle-based approach to how their minds work.

Chantal: Can you tell me about your early career and what led you to learn about the inside>out principles.

Cheryl: I brought many years of experience to my role as a senior practitioner in Employee Training and Organizational Development at BAE Systems in the late '90s. Over the next decade, I was fortunate to be involved in leading and co-facilitating a series of Executive Institutes, where we taught over 1,000 leaders about the inside>out nature of the mind. The aim was to show them how, through having their own insights, they could improve and transform their leadership capability and potential in areas including leading change, building relationships, holding people accountable, mentoring and coaching.

Chantal: I understand you completed an EdD in 2005. What was the focus of your research?

Cheryl: It focused on the relationship between those leadership teams who experienced the State of Mind Leadership training institutes and organisational success. The profound changes in leadership style and the example they set had an immediate impact on the entire division. From a financial perspective, this was very good news – because it meant that not everyone needed to attend a seminar to get beneficial results.

I remember one leader who was brilliant but often overly critical and angry. When he realised that his reactions to people and situations were coming from his own perceptions through old habits of thinking, he calmed down and quickly began to notice huge benefits in his personal and professional life. He said, 'I used to be angry all the time and now it's just gone.'

Chantal: How did learning about this new paradigm benefit you personally?

Cheryl: I clearly remember my first personal insight and the lasting impact on my life. During a 1–1 learning retreat with Dr Dicken Bettinger, I had an epiphany about self-judgment. I realised I saw the world through a lens of judgemental thought – about myself and others. It was so ingrained I hadn't ever seen it. I never lived up to my own personal standards and it was painful. I didn't know back then that those standards were made up. It all looked so real and fixed. I remember Dicken saying that when you don't understand the power of *Thought*, you look around for the source of the pain in your hand, not realising that you are holding the hammer in the other.

Now, when I drift into being unnecessarily hard on myself or others, it doesn't feel good . . . it doesn't feel right. But before the insight, it looked normal and justified. When I realised that everyone (even myself) is responding based on how the world looks to them in the moment, I was naturally more compassionate. I became known as someone who enjoyed working with 'difficult' people because I didn't see them as difficult. I listened without judging them and they were able to mentally settle and see something new.

Chantal: How did your approach to working with clients change after you began learning about the inside>out psychology?

Cheryl: By the time I left BAE to start my own consulting business, I had abandoned most of the tools and techniques I had learned earlier in my career. They just didn't feel relevant anymore. One example is a popular time management tool that I was certified to teach. This tool included a simple step-by-step ranking process. For some people, it was the answer to their prayers. They loved it. But others told me it made them feel overwhelmed and hopeless. To them it was proof that they were overworked and unappreciated. I was puzzled! Was I missing something in how I was teaching it? Were some people just not getting it? But when you consider this through the inside>out lens, you realise that there's no right way to manage time and no universal formula for the perfect work/life balance.

There are only so many hours in the day. How we relate to time and to our tasks and priorities is entirely subjective. So we must each decide what we're going to do and what we're not going to do. It's not that we can't prioritise. The problem is that we take on too much, or we don't ask for help. Then we get insecure or overwhelmed and we can't think clearly. We have to see what's stopping us from saying no . . . or what's stopping us from delegating work. And this always leads back to our own perceptions. For example, we worry about what people will think or we assume what's possible before we've checked it out. It always comes back to mental clarity and self-confidence and they are both an inside job.

Chantal: Talking about confidence, what have you seen about this over the years?

Cheryl: A lack of self-confidence is really the experience of feeling insecure. It manifests in many ways – not speaking up in meetings, avoiding certain conversations, taking on crazy amounts of work because saying no might look weak, not asking for help or staying in roles or situations that are no longer serving us. What's so indicative of the insideout psychology is how the resumés of these (mostly) women are amazing. They're PhD scientists and researchers with degrees from top universities and significant professional achievements, yet they get consumed with self-doubt as much as the next person.

In the old days we would have asked people to list their achievements and positive traits or post affirmations like 'I'm enough' on their mirror or computer. But these are quick fixes that don't last because they don't get to the root of the issue. Whereas when you recognise the nature and power of *Thought*, you're less likely to take your insecure thinking so seriously which means that it loses its power. Once my clients grasp this, they're better able to recognise when their mind is getting the better of them and return to mental clarity.

It's incredibly rewarding to see people change how they approach their work and personal lives. Being able to connect deeply with clients and help them uncover their natural resilience and well-being is deeply fulfilling. Even though many of my friends are now retired, I cannot imagine not doing what I do.

Helen Sully is an occupational psychologist who works with organisations and leadership teams, with a focus on change, culture and mental well-being. She is also a graduate of the Conscious Leadership School's inaugural two-year programme.

Chantal: What initially led you to explore this new direction?

Helen: I'd been working in a large corporate company for 12 years as a business psychologist, specialising in leading change and transformation. I loved what I was doing but felt ready for something different. I just didn't know what it was. By chance, I responded to what I thought was a job ad. I remember on our first call you said, 'This isn't a job but it will help you know what you want and how to get there.' And I ended up on the most amazing course of my life. I've never looked back. And that was eight years ago. And guess what? In the second month, I realised that all my ideas about security were made up. Little did I know how this would shape my next career move and change my life.

Chantal: When we first met, I was struck when you said that through all the years of psychology training, you were never taught about how we actually have experience, which is something we focus on in the Conscious Leadership School. Can you say more about this?

Helen: Yes, although having gained a degree in psychology, a Master's degree in occupational psychology, and becoming chartered, what hit me about the Inside>out principles, is how they explain the origin of mental experience, for all humans. Psychology has traditionally focused on neurology and cognition to explain behaviour. And it centres on the content of what we think and feel and the relationship between these two things. I realised the key to understanding behaviour and change is to understand the origin of feelings and perceptions; the principles that shape our entire reality.

So, while I wasn't actively seeking this, it has completely transformed my professional and personal life. And in terms of leadership, organisational culture, and change management, the inside>out psychology provides a universal framework to navigate and lead in these areas. By understanding the nature of human experience, I can better explain behaviour and make a more significant impact. It has so many powerful implications.

Chantal: How has this awareness impacted your life on a personal level?

IIclen: One of the biggest insights I had was realising that my thoughts are not facts. So when I was making a decision about starting my own business, and leaving something that seemed quite secure, safe and permanent, my thinking was based on fcar, risk and the unknown. If I didn't understand where those insecure feelings were coming from, I would have seen those thoughts or feelings as truth. Of course, there's some risk but I would have been deciding from a place of fear and would have taken a much more conservative approach, which is, 'I need to stay safe' . . . because it looked like safety was in 'permanence' and in what I already knew.

I had all these beliefs about what a permanent or secure work situation looked like and what it meant. If I hadn't seen that it was all made up, I wouldn't have left my job. It was a moment I'll never forget where it blew the lid off everything.

When you understand what your feelings mean, and what they don't mean, it puts you in a completely different position where you can make decisions from a place of clarity, not insecurity. So the end result was that I left my job and set up my own business. And I've been doing that for eight years. Yes, there were fears and concerns like 'you might not work . . . you've got a mortgage to pay, children and responsibilities'. But then you realise that if you try something, and it doesn't work, you can always change it. And I didn't think that way before. Whenever I was making a decision, I thought there was a right or a wrong, or just one or two options, which isn't true. You're always going to be gifted with options because the human mind is an ideas generator. And guess what, when something doesn't work, we've got the ability and opportunity to think of something new. But before this, it looked like you make a choice and that's it. It's fixed. So it was a much more rigid way of being, rather than this sea of opportunity that's always here . . . which is very nice to know.

Chantal: Absolutely. Sometimes people tell me they're unhappy in their job or relationships, for example. And you can hear that they feel like they have no choice. Living in the context of 'no choice' stops us from considering what could be and keeps us feeling stuck or trapped. It's hard to know what the true possibilities are unless we stand at the very edge of those imagined limits and take another look.

Helen: Yes, I love that. When you look at Covid, it's a great example of how industry got insightfully creative in just a matter of weeks. Because it blew the lid off any imagined boundaries. And everybody suddenly had to think differently, because the original way of operating was no longer viable. And that capability to adapt and change was always sat there, quietly waiting within every individual and every organisation. And we're now operating in a very different world because of it, which is fantastic for organisations that have introduced hybrid ways of working, giving people more flexibility in how they live and work. Whereas before, IT/leaders might have said, 'We could never risk having people working from home due to security/trust, etc.' and it would have taken six months or a year to make that change. But I saw first-hand how we had people set up to work from home within weeks. And we saw an increase in performance. My point is the capacity for transformation is always there because it lives in thought, in people's minds and hearts. If we don't fall into the trap of putting that lid on.

Chantal: How has this awareness influenced other aspects of your life?

Helen: I've got two children, 9 and 14. Being a parent and under-standing how my children experience reality – which is the same for all of us – is a completely different way of understanding their behaviour. Because when we don't understand the mechanics of the mind, we tend to interpret life through what we're seeing in front of us, through people's actions. But when you understand how the mind works, you know that behaviour is only one part of the jigsaw. You become more interested in and aware of what's behind behaviour. You have a lot more empathy and more understanding for yourself and for others because you realise we are all in the same boat . . . we're all thinking and feeling our way through life. From a parenting perspective, although I will go out of my way to protect them and care for them, I realise children have resilience and wis-dom built in as a default, which is a beautiful thing to know.

One striking example was when my son had a severe anaphylactic reaction while we were abroad. In the moment, I was able to admin-ister the EpiPen without hesitation. I don't know how but I just knew what to do. While my son was in intensive care, my head was full of thoughts about what a terrible parent I was, taking him half way across the world and letting him be in a situation that nearly killed him. But it was so helpful to remember that those feelings of guilt, shame and self-blame were passing thoughts, not truths. And that meant that I was able to sit in those feelings without trying to change them. This was huge . . . to know that it's OK to feel any-thing . . . it means you're not afraid of your own experience. And it was super helpful to know that, because we needed to make some decisions about how to proceed, based on what was truly best for my son and our family. We were only three days into a three-week trip. It was going to be a long onward journey for a 10-year-old who had just been through a life-threatening condition. In that moment,

I really believed that home = safety. This was a very strong idea in my mind, as in, 'I've got to go home because that's where he'll be safe.'

If I didn't understand what was happening in my mind, I could easily have acted from fear and just gone home. But we didn't, because eventually I saw that it was just an idea, not a fact. It's the same with my job, where the only option that seemed safe was to stay. And my son wanted to continue the journey. I saw his innate resilience, watching him laughing and enjoying life. I noticed that, unlike the adults around him, he wasn't overthinking the situation. He was just present. And there was a real moment as a parent, when I got to see how the mind works, not just for myself, but for everyone. It's a beautiful thing to see how someone can go through quite a traumatic experience and reset so quickly. And that's because he just didn't have much thinking about it. And we went on to have the most amazing experience as a family. When we got to Australia, of course, we were very careful with what we ate and where we went.

Then six months later we had profound proof that there is no ultimate 'safe' place as such for my son. I had a call from the school to say that they had given my son some eggs by accident. Thankfully he was OK. But it blew my mind because I always thought that school was one of the safest places he could be. Schools are trained on children's eating habits. You wear a big lanyard around your neck that says 'I'm allergic to xyz'. And somebody made a mistake. And I realised, wow, safety doesn't live in a particular location. It's not a place. And what I truly know is that resilience is our default. Now that's a safe pair of hands to be in! As long as we know not to think our way out of it.

I could be living in a place of fear, worrying about him eating something by accident. And I know a lot of people with severe allergies who, because of fearful thinking, are living with anxiety and a restricted life. And that doesn't mean you don't take sensible precautions. We always carry an EpiPen and there are certain places we don't eat. But I don't live in a place of fear. And neither does he, even though we live with his condition day in and day out.

That's quite different to how I would have been before I learned about the inside>out psychology. And that's the other thing. Thank goodness we carried an EpiPen that day. The beauty of the mind is that it allows you to plan. And the danger of the mind is that it allows you to overthink! And it's the same in work, and in business. The creativity of *Thought* means we can imagine and create new futures. The mind is brilliant for creating strategies. But when a person or a team overthinks or gets paralysed by setbacks and they don't understand what's happening psychologically, it massively restricts what they perceive as possible.

Chantal: What have you learned about change that has been most transformational?

Helen: The one thing we spend little time learning about as human beings is how we have this incredible natural capacity for insight. And it's the gateway to change and we've been having insights all our lives.

This is important for organisations. Teaching and instruction is great in certain contexts. But if we want real and lasting change, facilitate insight within a team and you'll get that long-term change, because people realise for themselves what is the right way or what is the best route to take.

The opportunity for new and fresh ideas is the biggest gift we can ever be given – and we all have the capacity for it! And whether that's as a parent or whether it's in decisions you make in your personal life, or in the direction of a company and how you're going to look after your employees . . . knowing that you're designed to have fresh, wise thinking . . . what more could you want?

And the best thing is how the benefits in the workplace and in our personal lives are the same. For example, people don't just get on better with their colleagues but they have better relationships with their partners, their children or their mother-in-law.

There are no limits to what we can learn and the impacts extend right across our lives.

Ami Chen Mills-Naim is an author, activist, mother of two, journalist and spiritual-psychological coach and mentor. Her father, Dr Roger Mills, was a pioneer in bringing this insideout understanding of the mind to schools, social services, governments and at-risk communities worldwide.

Chantal: Can you say a little about your background and how you were introduced to the inside>out psychology?

Ami: I consider myself incredibly fortunate to have been born into a family with a very caring and loving mother and very adventurous father, who helped found this psychology.

My parents divorced when I was three and my father, Dr Roger Mills, raised me a majority of the time. Through him, I had the opportunity to meet Mr Sydney Banks, who had a life-changing, spiritual insight in the 1970s. This insight revealed the essential role of the Principle of *Thought* in the human experience and the creation of human suffering.

Mr Banks later introduced the 'Three Principles' of *Mind, Consciousness* and *Thought* as the psycho-spiritual trinity governing all human perception and experience. I grew up around Mr Banks, my father and his colleagues.

Chantal: Can you describe the influence of Sydney Banks and your father's work on your early life?

Ami: My childhood was spent partly on Salt Spring Island, where Syd lived with his then-wife, Barb. It was an incredible, very natural, very beautiful environment. I was surrounded by loving, generous and wise individuals discovering the depths of their own connection to organic wisdom and truth.

Growing up partially on the island, within this community, had a profound impact on me, which I realised most acutely when I left for college. I looked back at the people I grew up around (not just on the island, but in California and Florida too as my father travelled to establish this work) and realised how optimistic, kind, well-adjusted and grounded they were. I saw a lot of folks struggling in college with substances, addictions and dysfunctional family dynamics. This was an Ivy League college!

Chantal: Can you say more about your father, Dr Roger Mills, and the work he did in the community?

Ami: My father was a pioneer in the fields of psychology, community resilience and mental health. He was a courageous and rebellious person who sought to explore and expand the frontiers of his field. He dedicated his life to helping individuals and communities recognise the innate resilience and wisdom within – they went on to transform their lives and the communities they lived in.

Chantal: Can you share some of the significant successes from his work in this area?

Ami: The most famous of these was the project at Modello and Homestead Gardens in South Dade County, Florida, memorialised in Prevention Author Jack Pransky's book, *Modello: A Story of Hope for the Inner City and Beyond*. This work, which involved US Attorney General Janet Reno (who was Attorney General for the state of Florida at the time) was also featured on *The Today Show* in the United States.

My father would go on to work in the Bronx, New York, LA, South San Francisco and Oakland's Coliseum Gardens. As a result of many of these projects, rates of violence and homicide went down dramatically and civic engagement, school attendance and academic achievement improved.[2] After we co-founded our non-profit, the Center for Sustainable Change, we both went on to work in communities in Des Moines, Iowa; Charlotte, North Carolina and the Mississippi Delta with similar outcomes.

Chantal: One of the things I've noticed over the years is how you have always followed your heart in terms of your work. Can you say a little about how your career evolved?

Ami: In my twenties, I worked as a journalist and wrote an article questioning the media's message regarding depression and the rise of 'new' SSRI medications (Prozac, etc.). I was curious about the complete omission of the human spirit in this narrative.

During my research, I interviewed 'depressed' individuals, my father's colleagues, psychiatrists and major authors. It was during this time I realised I wanted to have a more direct impact on people who were suffering deeply in life. Soon after, I left journalism as my main line of work.

Chantal: Can you tell me about your involvement in the Inside>out principles' educational efforts and your subsequent work in county jails and other institutions?

Ami: In 1996, I enrolled in an intensive training and certification program based on the principles you speak of. This program was provided by Santa Clara Valley's Health and Hospital System in Santa Clara County, actually where Silicon Valley is. After graduating, I was recruited by Barbara Faye Sanford, then Director of 'Health Realization Services'. She hired me to teach in the county jails, juvenile hall, schools and work furlough programs. I also led 'core courses' for county employees and conducted training for specific departments. Additionally, I had the opportunity to collaborate with my father on community programs in San Francisco and the Bronx.

Chantal: Tell me about the non-profit that you helped to set up. What were your responsibilities as executive director?

Ami: In 2004, with my father, I launched the Center for Sustainable Change, a non-profit organisation dedicated to expanding his work in communities across the country. Together, we built relationships with various Bay Area-based foundations, schools and government agencies. We also partnered with the W.K. Kellogg Foundation and the Shinnyo En Foundation to implement the National Community Resiliency Project (NCRP). As executive director, I was responsible for overseeing the organisation's operations, conducting training and raising funds for Principles-based, innate resilience programs across the United States.

Chantal: I remember us sorting through your father's papers and projects. It was inspiring to see how much work had been done and all those who tirelessly gave their time and love to this work. What were some of the most significant and memorable successes from these projects?

Ami: I wrote a two-year report for the Kellogg Foundation called 'Awakening the Beloved Community' about this work – that phrase is based on Dr Martin Luther King's vision for humanity. What we saw included decreased symptoms of stress, anxiety and depression. A significant fall in crime and violent assault. Greater cooperation between police and residents. Less stress and health symptoms at work. Overall, a general feeling of tremendous receptivity and accompanying insights from nearly all participants in communities. I found that very gratifying. But that is also fairly typical, as I learned from my work in Santa Clara County. People hear truth and they resonate. Especially when they are being directed to their innate wisdom.

Chantal: You became involved in climate activism – how did this happen and what do you see as the role of innate resilience in social and political activism and change?

Ami: In 2019, I read the online paper 'Deep Adaptation'[3] by Professor Jem Bendell from the University of Cumbria. I am not currently a fan of Bendell, but this paper affected me greatly.

I immediately became a lobbyist for Citizens Climate Lobby in the US, travelled to Washington DC to meet with Congresspeople and helped found the Santa Cruz Chapter of Extinction Rebellion, US. In addition, I served on the International Regenerative Cultures Working Group for XR, bringing the Principles to this global climate activism group.

My current focus is on bridging spiritual principles with social, political and ecological activism. We live in dire and troubling times. We need our best thinking and our deepest wisdom to navigate the storm and to bring our ships of state into calm harbour.

Chantal: Could you share more about your political involvement and your efforts to bring climate issues to the forefront of people's consciousness?

Ami: In 2022, I ran for local political office with the aim of bringing climate issues to the forefront of community conversations, even though my chances for winning were slim. It was an opportunity for me to engage with the community and raise awareness about the urgent need for action on the climate crisis and racial justice and equity. Through my continued, local and national political involvement, through my journalism in radio and podcasts, blog sites and social media, I hope to create meaningful dialogue and inspire collective action.

Chantal: What is it about this work that seems so important?

Ami: I believe that integrating spiritual principles with social, political and ecological activism is crucial for creating positive change in the world at this tipping-point moment in human history.

By recognising the innate resilience within each of us and fostering our connection to wisdom and truth, we can – *I pray* – collectively address the many challenges we face. I have been dismayed by a common spiritual 'myth' that politics is for 'others' not for 'spiritual people'. That was not true for Martin Luther King, Jr and so many religious and simply loving and spiritual Black activists in this country. That is not true for Native American activists fighting the fossil fuel industry. That was not true for Gandhi. It is simply not true.

I am grateful for the opportunities I've had to contribute to transformative work and find myself still committed to making a difference in people's lives and in our relationships with one another and the planet.

This spiritual understanding has enabled me to act without attachment and without very much ego or personal resentment. I do not know what the future holds. I only know that we can each do our best for life on Earth, in the world of form. Why not?

Personal reflections

What a time to be alive. There are so many challenges and possibilities that demand our collective attention, creativity, courage, and compassion. And it can so easily seem as if they are separate issues or 'not relevant to my life,' but they're all connected, and will touch all of our lives.

Most of us will be called to the edge of our known capabilities and knowledge. There will be discomfort and suffering. Do we stick our heads in the sand? Do we distract ourselves and look away? Or do we lean in and uncover the best parts of ourselves?

Thankfully, all the insight and wisdom we need for a better world is already inside. It's the aha moment when clarity comes. It's the quiet (or loud) inner voice that nudges us to take action. It's the instinctive push that propels you to act in the face of injustice, and that deep sense of compassion and kinship that we feel without even trying.

Each one of us has a unique part to play in the game of life. Each of us can be a catalyst for change. We can empower those around us and amplify important voices that are marginalised or less visible. We can take care of each other. The light that lives inside us will always be brighter than any darkness or fear.

Resilient communities are created when we can speak honestly, share our fears and concerns, rally together, laugh together, challenge and hear each other, and acknowledge the unique experiences and perspectives that enrich our understanding of the world. That's how we address the root causes of our most pressing issues and create a beautiful world that works for everyone. Together.

As Margaret Mead said, "Never doubt that a small group of thoughtful, committed citizens can change the world; indeed, it's the only thing that ever has."

With Love,
Chantal

Author's acknowledgements

My endless gratitude to Keith Blevens PhD, Valda Monroe and Christina Hall PhD for your mentoring, friendship and wise counsel over so many years.

Thank you to Cheryl for your consistent presence as a colleague, friend, cheerleader and reader of many re-writes. Thank you to Mary for our inspiring and insightful conversations while walking in nature. Thanks to Debi and Cris for sharing feedback that highlighted important blind spots.

Thank you to Monique for your unconditional wisdom and love.

My deep appreciation for Sydney Banks and for all you big hearted practitioners, pioneers and change makers who help to uncover compassion and wisdom.

Thank you to all my friends, clients and colleagues, from whom I learn so much every day.

Author's acknowledgements

My heartfelt appreciation for everyone who shared their stories and agreed to be part of this book, including Khalil Ibrahimi, Nick Hammond, Nick Burrows, Zoe Patrick, Hannah Carter, Chris Ingham, Justin Martin, Claudette Parry Laws, Giles Abbott.

Thank you to my publisher who helped to make this book possible.

And of course Andrew who has been a 'book widow' for quite some time (again), but remained steadfast in his support, love and patience. Thank you!

Publisher's acknowledgements

Text credits

xx Jiddu Krishnamurti: Quoted by Jiddu Krishnamurti; xxii Vishnu Purana: Quoted by Vishnu Purana, Indian Wisdom; 3 Mark Twain: Quoted by Mark Twain; 5 American Psychological Association: Masten, A.S. (2001) 'Ordinary magic: Resilience processes in development'. American Psychologist. 56(3), 227–38; 7 James Davies: From Twitter, 17 January 2021 @JDaviesPhD; 11 Philip K. Dick: Quoted by Philip K. Dick; 14 Marilyn L Bowman: Marilyn L Bowman, retired as Prof. Emerita from the Department of Psychology, Simon Fraser University. Retreived from https://www.researchgate.net/profile/Marilyn-Bowman; 15 Anil Seth: Quoted by Anil Seth; 22 Sydney Banks: Quoted by Sydney Banks, The Missing Link; 24 Sydney Banks: Quoted by Sydney Banks; 24 Virginia Wolfe: Quoted by Virginia Wolfe; 25 Erwin Schrödinger: Quoted by Erwin Schrödinger; 25 Sydney Banks: Quoted by Sydney Banks; 27 David Bohm: Quoted by Professor David Bohm, Physicist and author; 28 Max Planck: Quoted by Max Planck; 29 Sydney Banks: Quoted by Sydney Banks; 29 Christof Koch: Quoted by Christof Koch; 33 Henry David Thoreau: Quoted by Henry David Thoreau; 34 Archie Williams: Quoted by Archie Williams; 40 Michelangelo: Quoted by Michelangelo; 40 Rory Mclroy: Quoted by Rory Mclroy; 41 Steven Kotler: Quoted by Steven Kotler; 43 The

National Library of Australia: Watts, Alan, 1915–1973. (1954). The wisdom of insecurity. New York: Pantheon; 47 Donald Hoffman: Quoted by Donald Hoffman; 51 Valda Monroe: Quoted by Valda Monroe; 57 Alan Watts: Quoted by Alan Watts; 65 Sydney Banks: Quoted by Sydney Banks, The Missing Link; 66 William James: William James: The Varieties of Religious Experience lecture 1, p. 16; 67 Carl Sagan: Quoted by Carl Sagan; 73 John Milton: Quoted by John Milton; 75 Adyashanti: Quoted by Adyashanti; 76 Bill Pettit: Quoted by Dr. Bill Pettit; 80 World Health Organisation: Doing What Matters in Times of Stress: An Illustrated Guide, World Health Organisation, Retrieved from https://apps.who.int/iris/bitstream/handle/10665/331901/9789240003910-eng.pdf; 82 Jim Carrey: Quoted by Jim Carrey; 93 George Berkeley: Quoted by George Berkeley (1685–1753); 94 Ludwig Wittgenstein: Quoted by Ludwig Wittgenstein; 99 David Bohm: Quoted by Professor David Bohm; 100 Ronald David Laing: Quoted by Ronald David Laing; 103 Salman Rushdie: Quotes by Salman rushdie; 104 Kurt Vonnegu: Quotes by Kurt Vonnegu; 105 Albert Einstein: Quotes by Albert Einstein; 107 Werner Ehrhart: Quotes by Werner Ehrhart; 107 Portfolio: Dr. Benjamin Hardy (2020), Personality Isn't Permanent: Break Free from Self-Limiting Beliefs and Rewrite Your Story, Portfolio; 109 Carl Jung: Quotes by Carl Jung in 1921; 116 Gary Younge: Quotes by Gary Younge; 112 David Bohm: Quotes by David Bohm; 112 Portfolio: Dr. Benjamin Hardy (2020), Personality Isn't Permanent: Break Free from Self-Limiting Beliefs and Rewrite Your Story, Portfolio; 112 Adam M. Grant: Quotes by Professor Adam M. Grant.; 114 Bruce Harold Lipton: Quotes by Bruce Harold Lipton; 114 Dr James Davies PhD: Quotes by Dr James Davies PhD; 119 Christof Koch: Quotes by Christof Koch; 120 Dr. Jill Bolte-Taylor: Quotes by Dr. Jill Bolte-Taylor; 121 George Bernard Shaw: Quotes by George Bernard Shaw; 123 William James: Quotes by William James; 124 George Bernard Shaw: Quotes by George Bernard Shaw; 132 Robert Anton Wilson: Quotes by Robert Anton Wilson; 137 Emily Atack: Quotes by Emily Atack; 140 Carl Sagan: Quotes by Carl Sagan; 149 Sydney Banks: Quotes by Sydney Banks; 149 William James: Quotes by William James; 151 Jiddhu Krishnamutri: Quotes by

Jiddu Krishnamurti; 151 Byron Kathleen Mitchell: Quotes by Byron Kathleen Mitchell; 154 Deeyah Khan: Deeyah Khan; 155 Deeyah Khan: Deeyah Khan; 159 Rumi: Quotes by Rumi; 161 William James: Quotes by William James; 163 Elizabeth Gilbert: Quotes by Elizabeth Gilbert; 166 Elisabeth Kübler Ross Foundation: Interview by Dr. Elisabeth Kübler-Ross, Retrieved from https://www.youtube.com/watch?v=0kR8VianhSk. [Accessed: 6 September 2023.]; 166 Dr. Elisabeth Kübler-Ross: Quotes by Dr. Elisabeth Kübler-Ross; 168 Basic Books: George A. Bonanno, (2010), The Other Side of Sadness: What the New Science of Bereavement Tells Us About Life After Loss, Basic Books.; 169 Dr. Elisabeth Kübler-Ross: Quotes by Dr. Elisabeth Kübler-Ross; 169 Elizabeth Gilbert: Quotes by Elizabeth Gilbert; 169 American Psychological Association, Inc: Bonanno, G. A. (2004). Loss, Trauma, and Human Resilience: Have We Underestimated the Human Capacity to Thrive After Extremely Aversive Events? American Psychologist, 59(1), 20–28. doi:10.1037/0003-066x.59.1.20; 172 Aldous Huxley: Quotes by Aldous Huxley; 179 Louisa May Alcott: Quotes by Louisa May Alcott; 181 William Shakespeare: Quotes by William Shakespeare; 191 Helen Keller: Quotes by Helen Keller; 193 John Allen Paulos: Quotes by John Allen Paulos; 196 Donald Hoffman: Quotes by Professor Donald Hoffman; 200 Deepak Chopra LLC.: Quotes by Deepak Chopra; 202 Sydney Banks: Quotes by Sydney Banks; 202 Nelson Mandela: Quotes by Nelson Mandela; 205 Ralph Waldo Emerson: Quotes by Ralph Waldo Emerson.

Image credits

COV Getty Images: StarLineArts/iStock/Getty Images; 18 Shutterstock: Zimniy/Shutterstock; 160 Shutterstock: KenshiDesign/Shutterstock.

About the author

Chantal Burns is an experienced coach, speaker and author of best-selling book *Instant Motivation* which has been translated in to several languages.

The Conscious Leadership School, which was set up by Chantal, aims to empower individuals, leaders and teams to break free from mental constraints by removing interference. With a free mind we can make better decisions, and lead with clarity, compassion and courage in our personal and professional lives.

As well as being passionate about supporting organisations, Chantal provides mentoring for coaches, counsellors and educators.

With a depth of experience spanning over three decades, Chantal has established herself as a thought leader in conscious leadership, performance and emotional resilience.

Deeply committed to local community resilience, Chantal leads and participates in various initiatives, from setting up a thriving community choir through to mental health and environmental projects.

To connect with Chantal on social media, search for
@chantalburnsauthor

For individual support, non-corporate work, speaking engagements, writing assignments: https://www.chantalburns.com/contact

For organisational coaching and development, speaking engagements, consulting or research: https://www.consciousleadershipschool.com/contact

To connect on LinkedIn: https://uk.linkedin.com/in/chantalburns
For all other enquiries: hello@chantalburns.com

Notes

What this book is *not* about

1 Krishnamurti, J. (2010, 1st edn 1969) Freedom from the Known. Rider.

1 The resilience myth

1 https://unnaturalcauses.org/assets/uploads/file/ OrdinaryMagic.pdf [Accessed: 4 September 2023.]
2 Masten, A.S. (2001) 'Ordinary magic: Resilience processes in development'. American Psychologist. 56(3), 227–38.
3 From Twitter, 17 January 2021 @JDaviesPhD.
4 Citation; Sutker, P.B., Davis, J.M., Uddo, M. and Ditta, S.R. (1995) 'War zone stress, personal resources, and PTSD in Persian Gulf War returnees'. Journal of Abnormal Psychology. 104(3), 444–52. Available at: https://doi.org/10.1037/0021-843X.104.3.444. [Accessed: 4 September 2023.]

2 It's an inside>out world

1 https://pubmed.ncbi.nlm.nih.gov/14736317/ [Accessed: 10 November 2023.]
2 Research into resilience in children includes: Garmezy, 1991; Luthar, Doernberger and Zigler, 1993; Masten, 2001; Rutter, 1987.
3 Marilyn L Bowman, retired as Prof. Emerita from the Department of Psychology, Simon Fraser University. Retrieved from https://www.researchgate.net/profile/Marilyn-Bowman
4 Bowman, M. (2016) Individual Differences in Posttraumatic Response: Problems with the adversity-distress connection. Routledge.
5 Figley 1999 / APA 2013.
6 Burns, C. (2015) Instant Motivation; the surprising truth behind what really drives top performance. Pearson.
7 https://www.ted.com/talks/anil_seth_your_brain_hallucinates_your_conscious_reality [Accessed: 10 November 2023.]
8 https://www.ncbi.nlm.nih.gov/pmc/articles/PMC4172306/ and https://pubmed.ncbi.nlm.nih.gov/18303940. https://www.nature.com/articles/d41586-021-02939-z [Accessed: 4 September 2023.]
9 State of Mind at Work Survey 2014.
10 Banks, S. (2012) Missing Link: Reflections on philosophy and spirit. International Human Relation Consultants.
11 https://www.deepdyve.com/lp/springer-journals/experience-teaches-plants-to-learn-faster-and-forget-slower-in-0ZgFoH4IWe and https://www.newyorker.com/magazine/2013/12/23/the-intelligent-plant [Accessed: 4 September 2023.]
12 Simon Garner, World Science Festival, https://www.youtube.com/watch?v=RpwW9Lw2Ku4 [Accessed: 4 September 2023.]

3 How to reset and return to sanity

1 https://www.esquire.com/sports/a36820863/rory-mcilroy-mental-health-interview/ [Accessed: 10 November 2023.]

2 Watts, A. (1951). *The Wisdom of Insecurity: A Message for an Age of Anxiety.* Vintage. [Accessed: 10 November 2023.]

3 Klotz, L. (2021) Subtract: The untapped science of less. St Martin's Press.

4 https://www.livinginthetimeofdying.com/about [Accessed: 10 November 2023] and https://shoutout.wix.com/so/b0OfT-ga4U?languageTag=en [Accessed: 10 November 2023.]

5 https://youtu.be/3MvGGjcTEpQ?si=NBIgRMqblq8gvVIW [Accessed: 10 November 2023.]

6 Adapted from the pioneering work of Dr Keith Blevens and Valda Monroe. https://threeprinciplespsychology.com/ [Accessed: 10 November 2023]

4 Why positive thinking is outdated

1 Adapted and inspired by Watzlawick, P., Weakland, J. H., & Fisch, R. (1974). *Change: Principles of problem formation and problem resolution.* W. W. Norton.

2 BBC Women's Hour radio interview between Anita Rani and Brene Brown via BBC Sounds https://www.bbc.co.uk/sounds/play/m001219m [accessed September 2023]

3 William James: The Varieties of Religious Experience lecture 1, p. 16.

4 Author of Pale Blue Dot (1995) Film Pale Blue Dot: A Vision of the Human Future in Space (1994). Carl Sagan was a scientist, author and documentary maker who received the NASA medals for Exceptional Scientific Achievement.

5 Freedom from stress, anxiety and burnout

1 https://www.who.int/mental_health/evidence/burn-out/en/. [Accessed: 5 September 2023.]

2 https://www.hse.gov.uk/statistics/causdis/stress.pdf. [Accessed: 5 September 2023.]

3 ADAA, 2020.

4 https://www.freyaindia.co.uk/p/why-are-so-many-girls-on-ssris. [Accessed: 5 September 2023.]

5 https://pharmaceutical-journal.com/article/news/number-of-young-children-prescribed-antidepressants-has-risen-by-41-since-2015 [Accessed: 5 September 2023.]

6 Adyashanti (2009) The End of Your World: Uncensored straight talk on the nature of enlightenment. Sounds True Inc.

7 https://www.youtube.com/watch?v=ft3eujiQxzs [Accessed 13 November 2023.] https://drbillpettit.com/ [Accessed 13 November 2023.]

8 Doing what matters in times of stress: an illustrated guide. Geneva: World Health Organization; 2020.

9 https://time.com/collectionpost/3894477/david-foster-wallace-commencement-speech/ From commencement speech at Kenyon College Graduation ceremony. Ohio. [Accessed: 5 September 2023.]

10 https://www.youtube.com/watch?v=V80-gPkpH6M [Accessed: 10 November 2023.]

11 Monty Python https://youtu.be/0-9qZ4Zs6Ys. [Accessed: 5 September 2023.]

12 https://www.theguardian.com/education/2023/mar/21/ruth-perry-ofsted-regime-fatally-flawed-says-family-of-headteacher-who-killed-herself [Accessed: 5 September 2023.]

13 https://www.headteacher-update.com/content/news/ruth-perry-death-ofsted-must-listen-to-coroner-recommendations/

14 https://www.nytimes.com/2018/09/18/opinion/wittgensteins-confession-philosophy.html [Accessed: 10 November 2023.]

15 Bohm, D. (1st edn 1994) Thought as a System (2nd edn.) Routledge/Taylor & Francis.

16 Burns, C. (2015) State of mind at work study.

17 Goleman, D. (1998) Vital Lies, Simple Truths The psychology of self deception. Bloomsbury Publishing.

6 The myth of me

1   Vonnegut, K. 1982 Deadeye Dick. New York: Delacorte Press/Seymour Lawrence

2   http://www.wernererhard.com/ [Accessed: 10 November 2023.]

3   Hardy, B. (2020) Personality Isn't Permanent. Penguin Random House.

4   Sources include: 'Measuring the MBTI ... And Coming Up Short', Journal of Career Planning and Employment, 1993. 54: pp. 48–53; '... across a 5-week retest period, 50% of the participants received a different classification on one or more of the (MBTI) scales', 'Cautionary Comments Regarding the Myers-Brigg Type Inventory', Consulting Psychology Journal: Practice and Research, summer; https://journals.sagepub.com/doi/abs/10.1177/014920639602200103. [Accessed: 5 September 2023]; Dr Pittenger 1993 and 2005 'Several studies, however, show that even when the test-retest interval is short (e.g., 5 weeks), as many as 50 percent of the people will be classified into a different type. This is to say that the test fails to meet standards of "test-retest" reliability.' 'Measuring the MBTI ... And Coming Up Short', Journal of Career Planning and Employment, 1993. 54: p. 48–53.

5   https://www.livingiseasy.com.au/podcasts/bruce-lipton-1/#:~:text=Then-you-find-out-oh-our beliefs-our-perceptions [Accessed: 10 November 2023.] https://www.ncbi.nlm.nih.gov/pmc/articles/PMC6438088/ [Accessed 10 November 2023.]

6   https://www.doubledown.news/watch/2023/july/27/garyyounge-demolishes-identity-politics-and-myth-of-race [Accessed 10 November 2023.]

7   Sacks, O. (1985) The Man Who Mistook His Wife for a Hat. Gerald Duckworth.

8   https://www.newscientist.com/article/mg25634192-600-will-2023-be-the-year-we-finally-understand-consciousness/ [Accessed 10 November 2023.]

9   Bolte Taylor, J. (2008) My Stroke of Insight: A brain scientist's personal journey. Penguin Putnam.
10 ZOOM by Istvan Banyai.

7 Courageous conversations

1   Sample size 1,750 completions of SOMi – State of Mind Index.
2   'Asking for it?', available at: https://www.bbc.co.uk/programmes/m001hs5v. [Accessed: 15 September 2023.]
3   Source: Frances J. Milliken, Elizabeth W. Morrison, and Patricia F. Hewlin and was published in the Academy of Management Journal in 2003. The title of the study is 'An Exploratory Study of Employee Silence: Issues that Employees Don't Communicate Upward and Why'.
4   Katie, B. (2002) Loving What Is: Four questions that can change your life. Harmony.
5   Interview between Simon Sinek and documentary maker Deeyah Khan https://simonsinek.com/podcast/episodes/extreme-listening-with-deeyah-khan/ [Accessed 10 November 2023.]

8 Grief, loss and the true healer

1   Interview with Dr. Elisabeth Kübler-Ross, Retrieved from https://www.youtube.com/watch?v=0kR8VianhSk. [Accessed: 6 September 2023.]
2   Bonanno, G. (2009) The Other Side of Sadness: What the new science of bereavement tells us about life after loss. Basic Books
3   Bonanno, G. A. (2004). Loss, Trauma, and Human Resilience: Have We Underestimated the Human Capacity to Thrive After Extremely Aversive Events? American Psychologist, 59(1), 20–28. doi:10.1037/0003-066x.59.1.20

4   American Psychiatric Association (2022) The Diagnostic and Statistical Manual of Mental Disorders, Fifth Edition, Text Revision (DSM-5-TR). APA.

5   Huxley, A. (1952) Tomorrow and Tomorrow and Tomorrow. New York: Harper & Bros.

6   Channel 4 (2021) Caroline Flack: Her Life and Death.

9 You've got this!

1   www.mydadmrbrixton.com. [Accessed: 6 September 2023.]

2   Measure for Measure, Act 1, Scene 4.

3   https://www.chantalburns.com/blog-article/bbc-radio-london-interview-with-vanessa-feltz/

4   www.heartcommunitygroup.org. [Accessed: 6 September 2023.]

Voices from the field

1   Moncrieff, J. (2008). *The Myth of the Chemical Cure: A Critique of Psychiatric Drug Treatment*. Palgrave Macmillan.

2   http://www.amichen.com/community. [Accessed 7 September 2023.]

3   Bendell, Jem (2018) *Deep adaptation: a map for navigating climate tragedy*. Institute for Leadership and Sustainability (IFLAS) https://jembendell.com/2019/05/15/deep-adaptation-versions/ [Accessed November 2023.]

Index